HOW HIGH CAN YOU SCORE ON THIS 1975 PRO BASKETBALL QUIZ?

John Havlicek, the high-scoring forward who led the Boston Celtics to the NBA title last season, played ball at one of the following colleges:

> Boston College
> Ohio State
> Kentucky

Artis Gilmore of the Kentucky Colonels established an ABA single game record for rebounds in 1973-74. Did he haul down 25, 30 or 40?

Bob McAdoo of the Buffalo Braves paced the NBA in scoring last season. Did he average 33.9, 36.1 or 30.6 points?

Who was named a Coach of the Year in pro basketball in 1973-74 and then was fired at the end of the campaign?

One player is omitted here from the five who were named to the NBA final All-Star team last season . . . John Havlicek, Rick Barry, Kareem Abdul-Jabbar, Walt Frazier. Do you know which one it is?

Swen Nater of the San Antonio Spurs, who captured ABA rookie-of-the-year honors in 1973-74, is a native of a foreign country. Is he from Holland, Denmark or Sweden?

You'll find the answers to these and countless other questions in . . .

BASKETBALL STA

ABOUT THE AUTHORS

HAL BOCK has become one of the nation's most prolific authors of sports books. In addition to the co-authorship of FOOTBALL STARS OF 1974, two other recent books carry his byline. They are *The Big Whistle*, the story of hockey referee Bill Chadwick, and *Save! Hockey's Brave Goalies*. Bock is also a valued member of The Associated Press sports staff and has covered pro football's Super Bowl, baseball's World Series and hockey's Stanley Cup championship.

BEN OLAN also has a number of book credits, including editorship of *The 1974 Official Associated Press Sports Almanac* and *The Sports Immortals*. Olan is a contributing editor to *Sports Today*, the popular bi-monthly magazine, plus several other national magazines, including Pyramid's Sports Stars Series.

The authors wish to acknowledge the assistance of Nick Curran, public relations director of the National Basketball Association, Mike Recht, public relations director of the American Basketball Association, and Bert Rosenthal of The Associated Press for their help in the compilation of material used in this book.

BASKETBALL
STARS
OF 1975

by

Hal Bock and Ben Olan

PYRAMID BOOKS • NEW YORK

BASKETBALL STARS OF 1975

A PYRAMID BOOK

Pyramid edition published October, 1974

ISBN 0-515-03507-6

Library of Congress Catalog Card Number: 74-10450

Printed in the United States of America

Pyramid Books are published by Pyramid Communications, Inc. Its trademarks, consisting of the word "Pyramid" and the portrayal of a pyramid, are registered in the United States Patent Office.

Pyramid Communications, Inc., 919 Third Avenue, New York, N.Y. 10022

TABLE OF CONTENTS

THE SEASON PAST

NBA Season Past

The young players on the Boston Celtics were getting tired of hearing about the great Celtic teams of the past and the great Celtic traditions of the past. And at the outset of the 1973-74 National Basketball Association season, all the players on the club were determined to establish their own greatness and their own tradition.

They had heard about the legendary Bill Russell, the peerless defensive center and spiritual leader who had led the club to 11 NBA championships in 13 seasons, from the 1956-57 season to the 1968-69 campaign, when he retired. They had heard about the ballhandling wizardry of Bob Cousy, the deadly shooting of Bill Sharman, and the exploits of such other players as Sam Jones, K.C. Jones, Tom Heinsohn, Frank Ramsey, Jim Loscutoff and Tom Sanders. But few had experienced the basketball thrills of those stars, who had provided the Celtics with the greatest dynasty in pro basketball history.

Following Russell's retirement in 1969, Boston's pride, prestige and prominence plunged drastically. The Celtics even failed to make the playoffs the next two years, and their dynasty had crumbled.

Then they started putting the pieces together again. They won the Atlantic Division title in the 1971-72 season and again in 1972-73, but each time they were beaten by the New York Knicks in the playoffs, losing in the Eastern Conference final. In the second of those two seasons, General Manager Red Auerbach, the

coach and architect of Boston's championship teams of
the late 1950s and 1960s, blamed the playoff loss on
two prime factors: a double overtime setback that he
felt the officials "stole" from the Celtics during regula-
tion time, and an injury to captain John Havlicek,
which kept him out of one game and severely curtailed
his effectiveness in several other games.

Havlicek was the last main link between the old and
the new Celtics. He was the only member of the 1973-
74 club that had made a major contribution to Boston's
last championship in 1969. Two others—Don Nelson
and Don Chaney—also were on that team, but they
had played bit parts. In fact, everyone on that club was
overshadowed by the magnificent Bill Russell.

Now, they had been significantly rebuilt. Coach Heinsohn's starting lineup had Havlicek and Nelson at
forwards, Dave Cowens at center, and Chaney and Jo
Jo White at guards. The bench also was strong, with
Paul Silas, Paul Westphal, Steve Kuberski, Artie Williams, Henry Finkel, and rookies Phil Hankinson and
Steve Downing.

Basically, it was Havlicek's team. Unquestionably,
the others were significant contributors, but he was the
catalyst. And he was fully aware of it.

"I started with this team being rebuilt," he said.
"They sort of look to me because I've been here 12
years."

The Celtics were a running team. When their fast
break was working, they could wear down any team in
the league. Their speed, resilience and durability were
unmatched.

And for those reasons, both Auerbach and Havlicek
predicted the Celtics would go all the way again—win
their 12th NBA championship—but their first without
Russell.

"I don't think New York [the defending champion]

or any other team in the NBA has better talent than we do," said Havlicek. "I think we're a great scoring team. When we run and move and hit the open man, we can put an awful lot of points on the board in a very short time. In fact, when we're in that kind of a streak, no rival team can really stop us. About all they can do is call a time out and hope we lose our momentum."

"I think all the ingredients are there for us to win," said Auerbach. "We've got good balance and the experience to go with it. All we have to do is put it together . . . and I think we will. We're mature and we're ready."

The Celtics certainly were ready. They built a big early-season lead over the injury-riddled Knicks in the Atlantic Division and coasted to their third consecutive division title, finishing seven games ahead of New York.

The biggest surprise in the division, however, was the strong third-place finish of the young Buffalo Braves. The Braves were paced by Bob McAdoo, the scoring champion with a 30.6 average and the field goal percentage leader at .547, and Rookie of the Year Ernie DiGregorio, the leader in both assists average (8.2) and free throw percentage (.902). Buffalo wound up its fourth season in the league with 42 victories after winning only 22, 22, and 21 in their first three years, and qualified for the "wild card" playoff spot in the Eastern Conference.

The other playoff spot in the East went to Central Division champion Capital. The Bullets, playing in their new arena at Largo, Maryland, breezed to the title, despite serious injuries to center Wes Unseld and guard Archie Clark. Their key man was Elvin Hayes, winner of his second NBA rebounding championship.

In the Western Conference, Milwaukee and Los Angeles each won division titles for the fourth straight season, but did it in contrasting fashion. The Bucks, behind Player of the Year Kareem Abdul-Jabbar, were in front virtually all the way in taking the Midwest championship, while the Lakers had to rally for the Pacific Division crown. Los Angeles overtook the stumbling Golden State Warriors in the final week of the season, despite the absence of Wilt Chamberlain, who had defected to the American Basketball Association prior to the season; despite a series of injuries to perennial All-Star guard Jerry West, and despite the loss of Jim McMillian, traded to Buffalo for seven-foot center Elmore Smith, the man who replaced Chamberlain.

The rebuilt Lakers also had Connie Hawkins, acquired from Phoenix for Keith Erickson in an early-season trade; Stan Love, obtained from the Bullets, and rookies Kermit Washington and Nate Hawthorne.

In other key deals, Buffalo got power forward Garfield Heard and seven-foot rookie Kevin Kunnert from Chicago for John Hummer, then sent Kunnert and Dave Wohl to Houston for Jack Marin and Matt Guokas; Milwaukee signed veterans Cornell Warner and Dick Garrett as free agents; Seattle purchased Hummer from Chicago, and in the most stunning deal of all, the Atlanta Hawks sent the league's No. 2 scorer, Pete Maravich, to the New Orleans franchise that will begin play this season. In return, New Orleans yielded numerous draft choices.

The other two playoff spots last season went to Chicago, the Midwest runner-up, five games behind Milwaukee, and the Detroit Pistons, third-place finishers in the Midwest, two games in back of the Bulls.

Ray Scott, who had led the Pistons to their winningest season in history (52 victories) and their first playoff berth in six years, was a popular choice as Coach of the Year.

Named to the All-Star team were Havlicek and Rick

Barry of Golden State at forwards, Jabbar at center, and Walt Frazier of New York and Gail Goodrich of Los Angeles at guards.

Among the other important developments during the season were the announcement by Commissioner Walter Kennedy that he would retire on June 1, 1975, when his contract expires, and the approval of an 18th franchise, New Orleans, for the 1974-75 season, balancing the conferences into nine-team units.

In the opening round of the playoffs, Boston, New York and Chicago barely survived, while only Milwaukee had an easy time.

The Celtics needed six grueling games against rejuvenated Buffalo before subduing the Braves. With the best-of-seven series deadlocked 2-2, the Celtics squeaked to a 100-97 victory in game five, then won the sixth game 106-104 on White's two free throws after the final buzzer. Buffalo Coach Jack Ramsay, however, argued vehemently that time had not run out when White was fouled and that the Braves should have had a chance to inbound the ball and possibly try another shot. His bitter protest was rejected.

The Knicks, playing erratically and unpredictably, managed to get past the Bullets, 4 games to 3, with the help of a reawakened Walt Frazier, a slow starter but strong finisher in the series, and the fizzling of Elvin Hayes, a sensation for the Bullets in the first six games but a dud in the critical seventh game.

Chicago had an even tougher time against Detroit, winning its four games in the seven-game set by a total of 12 points, with margins of one, two, four and five points, including a pulsating 96-94 score in the finale.

Milwaukee routed the tired and injured Lakers, 4 games to 1, winning each of the last two games by 22 points, although easing up in the last quarters.

Next, it was Boston against New York, and Milwau-

kee against Chicago. Both series ended rapidly. The
Celtics, spurred by the magnificent play of the inspired
Havlicek, ran the aging and ailing Knicks into the
ground, 4 games to 1, and the Bucks had only one
close game—a two-pointer—in sweeping four straight
games from the undermanned Bulls, who were playing
in the semifinals for the first time.

That set up a Boston-Milwaukee final, with the
Bucks getting what usually was regarded as the coveted
home-court advantage because they had won more
games during the regular season than the Celtics. But
this time, the home court was of little advantage.

In the opener at Milwaukee, the Celtics were able to
employ their patented fast break and upset the Bucks'
offense with harassing defensive tactics, doubling up on
the ballhandler and forcing the Western Conference
champions into a bundle of errors. Boston won handily,
98-83.

Milwaukee, playing the entire series without standout
guard Lucius Allen, sidelined with torn knee liga-
ments, regrouped in game two and outlasted the Celtics
in overtime, 105-96. Then they went to Boston, and
again it was a split, the Celtics winning the opener 95-
83 and the Bucks taking the next game, 97-89.

Defense continued to rule the series in game five,
with neither team going over the 100-point mark for the
third straight game as Boston prevailed 96-87, for its
second victory on the Bucks' court. But Milwaukee
stayed alive—barely—in game six at Boston, posting
its second triumph on the Celtics' court, 102-101, on
Jabbar's sky hook with three seconds remaining in the
second overtime. It was one of the tensest, hardest-
fought, most dramatic games in NBA playoff history,
and sent the series back to Milwaukee for the seventh
and deciding game.

Again, the Celtics did not care about the visitors'

disadvantage. They bolted to a 17-point lead midway in the third quarter, then virtually stood still as Milwaukee charged back to within three points in the first minute of the fourth period, before regaining their momentum and pulling away for a scintillating 102-87 victory.

"This is like a rebirth," exclaimed the 34-year-old Havlicek, selected as the Most Valuable Player in the final series, as he celebrated his seventh NBA championship with the Celtics but his first since 1969.

"The first championships were all in the old Celtic tradition," he added with a smile as champagne dribbled down his face. "But this is the start of a new tradition. This is the greatest—there's no doubt about it. The younger guys on the team really wanted this one to prove themselves. All they hear about in Boston is the old Celtic teams and the old Celtic traditions. Now they have their own tradition."

A poster in Auerbach's office perhaps told it best: "The Celtics Are Back."

There was no doubt about it.

NBA ALL STAR GAME

Stung by the previous season's 20-point loss, the National Basketball Association's Western Division All Stars gained a measure of revenge, defeating the East 134-123.

The West stars came ready to play, jumping off to an early 20-5 lead that the East never overcame. The West bulge ballooned to as many as 25 points, but before it was over, the East made a contest of it.

With a record crowd of 14,360 watching in the Seattle Coliseum, Detroit's Bob Lanier and Spencer Haywood, of the host Seattle SuperSonics, wore down the East stars. Lanier was the game's most valuable player with 24 points and 10 rebounds, and Haywood scored 23 and pulled down 11 rebounds.

The East crept to within three points with just over three minutes to play, but baskets by Milwaukee's Kareem Abdul-Jabbar and Los Angeles' Gail Goodrich, sandwiched around a Lanier block, helped the West stay in front.

The box score:

EAST (123): Havlicek 5 0-2 10; Hudson 5 2-2 12; Cowens 5 1-3 11; Frazier 5 2-2 12; Maravich 4 7-9 15; Hayes 5 2-3 12; McAdoo 3 5-8 11; White 6 1-3 13; DeBusschere 8 0-0 16; Chenier 3 1-2 7; Tomjanovich 2 0-0 4; Carr 0 0-0 0; Totals 51 21-34.

WEST (134): Barry 3 2-2 8; Walker 4 4-4 12; Abdul-Jabbar 7 0-0 14; Goodrich 9 0-0 18; Petrie 3 2-2 8; Wicks 5 6-10 16; Scott 0 2-2 2; Lanier 11 2-2 24; Haywood 10 3-3 23; Bing 2 1-1 5; Van Lier 0 0-0 0; Thurmond 2 0-1 4; Totals 56 22-27.

| East | 29 | 18 | 38 | 38 | —123 |
| West | 39 | 27 | 35 | 33 | —134 |

Fouled Out—None.

Total Fouls—East 23; West 23.

Attendance—14,360.

NBA MVP—ABDUL-JABBAR

Kareem Abdul-Jabbar, Milwaukee's huge center and the man who makes the Bucks such a formidable force in the National Basketball Association, won the Podoloff Trophy as the National Basketball Association's Most Valuable Player for 1973-74.

Abdul-Jabbar topped Bob McAdoo of Buffalo, the league's leading scorer and field goal percentage leader, 528 points to 451, in the 19th annual polling of NBA players.

Bob Lanier of Detroit, who has helped propel the

Pistons to more victories than achieved any other season in the club's history, came in third, with Boston's Dave Cowens, last year's winner, a distant fourth and Elvin Hayes of Capital, the NBA's top rebounder, fifth.

For Abdul-Jabbar, it was the third time in his brilliant five-year career that he has won the Podoloff Trophy. In 1971, when he was known as Lew Alcindor, he and Oscar Robertson led the Bucks to their first NBA crown and the big center won in a landslide and repeated in 1972.

This year he had 74 first-place votes, 41 second-place votes and 35 third-place votes. Balloting from 181 active players was awarded with five points for a first-place vote, three points for a second-place vote and one point for a third.

Bill Russell won five Most Valuable Player awards in his 13 years as Boston's great center, and Wilt Chamberlain won it four times. Abdul-Jabbar, who turned 27 on April 16, thus has a good chance to overtake both great centers in this category.

1973-74 NBA MVP VOTING

	Player, Team	1	2	3	Points
1.	Kareem Abdul-Jabbar, Milwaukee	74	41	35	528
2.	Bob McAdoo, Buffalo	60	39	34	451
3.	Bob Lanier, Detroit	37	59	33	395
4.	Dave Cowens, Boston	3	18	22	91
5.	Elvin Hayes, Capital	4	12	18	74
6.	Walt Frazier, New York	2	1	11	24
7.	Rick Barry, Golden State	0	2	4	10
8.	Nate Thurmond, Golden State	1	1	0	8
9.	John Havlicek, Boston	0	1	2	5
	Norm Van Lier, Chicago	0	1	2	5
11.	Dave Bing, Detroit	0	1	0	3
	Phil Chenier, Capital	0	1	0	3
	Clifford Ray, Chicago	0	1	0	3
	Dave DeBusschere, New York	0	0	3	3
	Gail Goodrich, Los Angeles	0	0	3	3
16.	Lucius Allen, Milwaukee	0	0	2	2
	Bob Love, Chicago	0	0	2	2
18.	Spencer Haywood, Seattle	0	0	1	1
	Clyde Lee, Golden State	0	0	1	1
	Pete Maravich, Atlanta	0	0	1	1
	Rudy Tomjanovich, Houston	0	0	1	1
	(Blanks)	0	3	6	15

NBA MVPs

1955-56 Bob Pettit, St. Lous	1966-67 Wilt Chamberlain, Philadelphia
1956-57 Bob Cousy, Boston	1967-68 Wilt Chamberlain, Philadelphia
1957-58 Bill Russell, Boston	1968-69 Wes Unseld, Baltimore
1958-59 Bob Pettit, St. Louis	1969-70 Willis Reed, New York
1959-60 Wilt Chamberlain, Phila.	1970-71 Lew Alcindor, Milwaukee
1960-61 Bill Russell, Boston	1971-72 Kareem Abdul-Jabbar,
1961-62 Bill Russell, Boston	Milwaukee
1962-63 Bill Russell, Boston	1972-73 Dave Cowens, Boston
1963-64 Oscar Robertson, Cincinnati	1973-74 Kareem Abdul-Jabbar,
1964-65 Bill Russell, Boston	Milwaukee
1956-66 Wilt Chamberlain, Philadelphia	

NBA ALL-STAR TEAM

Walt Frazier, talented seven-year veteran guard of the New York Knicks, was the leading vote-getter on the National Basketball Association's year-end All-Star Team. Frazier had 15,291 of a possible 17 votes in the 28th annual balloting of writers and broadcasters in the 17 NBA cities.

Joining him on the first team were John Havlicek of the NBA World Champion Boston Celtics and Rick Barry of the Golden State Warriors at forward, Kareem Abdul-Jabbar of the Milwaukee Bucks at center, and Gail Goodrich of the Los Angeles Lakers at guard.

The second team consisted of Elvin Hayes of the Washington Bullets and Spencer Haywood of the Seattle SuperSonics at forward, Bob McAdoo of the Buffalo Braves at center, Dave Bing of the Detroit Pistons and Norm Van Lier of the Chicago Bulls at guard.

For Frazier, this is the third time he has made first team, having also been selected in 1970 and 1972. He was the leading scorer on the Knicks this season, averaging 20.5 points a game, as well as ranking fourth in the NBA in assists at 6.9 per game and making first-team All-Defensive Team for the sixth straight time.

Each franchise city receives one full vote in the balloting and in rolling up the highest total of any player, Frazier had the honor of a unanimous vote in 11 of the 17 cities.

Abdul-Jabbar, who won the Podoloff Trophy as the Most Valuable Player for the third time in his great five-year career, had a vote count of 14.541. Havlicek received a vote of 12.214, Goodrich 11.028 and Barry 9.973.

Each member of the first team receives a check for $500 and each second-team choice gets $250.

This is the fourth straight year that Havlicek and Abdul-Jabbar have made first team. Havlicek, Boston's all-time leading scorer, also made second team five times and Abdul-Jabbar did it once.

Goodrich, who was fifth in the NBA in scoring average at 25.3, was honored on the first team for the first time in his nine-year career. This is the third such selection for Barry, who ranked in the top 10 in scoring, free throw percentage and steals.

McAdoo, the NBA's leading scorer at 30.6 per game in just his second pro season, was a second-team choice for the first time.

Haywood, who ranked ninth in scoring average, seventh in rebounding average and 11th in blocked shots, had made first team in 1972 and 1973. Elvin Hayes, the NBA's best rebounder this season, was a second-team choice for the second time.

Bing was a two-time first-team choice before his second-team selection this spring. He is Detroit's all-time leader in every category except rebounding and helped the club to its most successful season ever, including 52 victories and a playoff berth.

Van Lier, a five-year veteran who plays the game with all-out enthusiasm, received his first post-season all-round recognition this spring. In a league well-stocked with top-notch guards, his selection points out the respect the 27-year-old from St. Francis has achieved.

* * * NBA 1973-74 ALL-STAR TEAM * * *
FIRST TEAM

Player, Team	Pos.	Hgt.	Wgt.	Vote
John Havlicek, Bos.	F	6-5	205	12.214
Rick Barry, G.S.	F	6-8	220	9.973
Kareem Abdul-Jabbar, Milw.	C	7-2	232	14.541
Walt Frazier, N.Y.	G	6-4	205	15.291
Gail Goodrich, L.A.	G	6-1	175	11.028

SECOND TEAM

Player, Team	Pos.	Hgt.	Wgt.	Vote
Elvin Hayes, Wash.	F	6-9	235	9.407
Spencer Haywood, Sea.	F	6-8	230	8.206
Bob McAdoo, Buff.	C	6-10	210	6.593
Dave Bing, Det.	G	6-3	185	5.975
Norm Van Lier, Chic.	G	6-1	175	3.413

NBA COACH OF THE YEAR—SCOTT

Ray Scott, in his first full season as a head coach in the National Basketball Association, was named Coach of the Year.

The 35-year-old coach of the Detroit Pistons called the honor bestowed upon him by a panel of 51 writers and broadcasters in the 12th annual voting, "the greatest individual award that's ever happened to me. I'm pleased and excited. But awards like this don't come without a lot of people being involved."

Scott received 33 votes for Coach of the Year. Jack Ramsay, who coached Buffalo to its first ever playoff berth, was runner-up with 10 votes. Larry Costello of Milwaukee had four votes, Bill Sharman of Los Angeles three, and K.C. Jones of Capital received one.

Under Scott, The Pistons posted club records for most victories (52), most victories at home (29) and most victories on the road (23). They qualified for the playoffs for the first time since 1968, just the second time since 1963. And they extended the Chicago Bulls to seven exciting games before bowing out.

Scott, a 6-9 forward and part-time center in his playing days, was with Detroit from 1961 until partway into the 1966-67 season when he was traded to Baltimore. He closed out his NBA playing career with the Bullets in 1970.

Ray became assistant coach under Earl Lloyd in 1972, and after seven games of the 1972-73 season, was named to succeed Earl. Under Scott the Pistons won 38 games and lost 37 but failed to make the playoffs. This season, to say the least, was much more successful.

NBA—ALL DEFENSIVE TEAM

For the fourth straight year, the 17 NBA coaches named Dave DeBusschere their league's best defensive player. The 33-year-old forward of the New York Knickerbockers received 33 of a possible 34 points to head the sixth annual All-Defensive Team for 1973-74, announced Commissioner Walter Kennedy.

Joining the 6-6 forward are Boston's John Havlicek at forward with 17 points; Kareem Abdul-Jabbar of Milwaukee at center with 24 points; Norm Van Lier of Chicago at guard with 23 points; and a tie between Walt Frazier of New York and Chicago's Jerry Sloan for the other guard position with 22 points. Each coach's first team vote counts two points and each second team vote counts one point.

On the second team are Elvin Hayes of Capital with 11 points, Chicago's Bob Love with nine, at forward; Nate Thurmond of Golden State at center with 11; Don Chaney of Boston at guard with 12 and a tie between Dick Van Arsdale of Phoenix and Jim Price of Los Angeles with four points.

DeBusschere, a 12-year veteran who has appeared in eight All-Star Games, is one of the major reasons why the Knicks had the NBA's best defense this season. He has been the top vote-getting forward since the All-Defensive Team balloting began at the end of the 1968-69 season, his first as a Knick.

Two years ago he was named unanimously to the team, the only player ever so honored.

For Havlicek, this is the third straight year he has been a first-team forward. He also made second team in 1970 and 1971. Abdul-Jabbar, earlier named the Most Valuable Player in the NBA this season, made first-team All-Defensive Team for the first time in his five-year NBA career.

Van Lier also was making first team for the first time in his five-year career. Van Lier was instrumental in Chicago reaching the Western Conference finals against Milwaukee.

So was Sloan, a nine-year veteran who was named to the first team for the third time.

NBA ROOKIE TEAM

Ernie DiGregorio of Buffalo and Ron Behagen of Kansas City-Omaha were unanimous picks on the NBA All Rookie team announced by Commissioner Walter Kennedy.

DiGregorio, the Rookie of the Year who led the NBA in assists and free throw percentage, and Behagen, a rugged 6-9 forward from Minnesota, were named by all 17 NBA head coaches in the 12th annual balloting.

Also selected to the first team are Mike Bantom of Phoenix, who had 13 votes; John Brown of Atlanta, who had 11; and Capital's Nick Weatherspoon, who had 10.

The second team consisted of Atlanta's Dwight Jones, Bernie Fryer of Portland, Jim Brewer of Cleveland, Don (Slick) Watts of Seattle, and a three-way tie among Mike D'Antoni of Kansas City-Omaha, Derrick Dickey of Golden State and E.C. Coleman of Houston.

DiGregorio was named the rookie of the year in an earlier vote of writers and broadcasters in the 17 NBA cities. But in being tied as the top vote-getter on the All-Rookie Team, the six-footer from Providence College becomes the third straight Brave so honored. Bob McAdoo was the top vote-getter last year and Elmore Smith, now with Los Angeles, accomplished this in 1972.

DiGregorio had 661 assists in 81 games for an 8.2 per game average and shot .902 from the foul line.

Behagen, the seventh player selected on the first round of the 1973 College Draft, had more rebounds (567) than any rookie this season, and was second to Sam Lacey on the Kings in this department. He also scored 876 points for an 11.0 per game average.

Bantom, a 6-9 forward from St. Joseph's, was Phoenix's No. 1 draft pick. He scored 769 points, a 10.1 per game average, and 519 rebounds.

Brown, Atlanta's first-round pick along with Jones, had 717 points and 441 rebounds. Weatherspoon, the Bullets' top pick, scored 494 points and pulled down 397 rebounds.

ABA Season Past

The New York Nets started the 1973-74 American Basketball Association season as the youngest and least experienced team in the league.

At the outset, they played like it.

After winning four of their first five games, they went into a complete tailspin, losing nine straight games and plunging into last place in the Eastern Division with a 4-10 record.

At that point, rookie Coach Kevin Loughery's job appeared in jeopardy and it seemed the team's chances of being one of the four teams in the five-team division to qualify for the playoffs were dim. After all, Loughery had done little to distinguish himself in his first coaching venture, compiling a 5-26 record after succeeding Roy Rubin with the 1972-73 Philadelphia 76ers, the team that finished with the worst record (9-73) in pro basketball history. And the Nets also had done little to distinguish themselves that same 1972-73 season, compiling a miserable 30-54 record, although qualifying for the fourth and final playoff spot in the East.

But this was virtually a whole new team. There was the new coach, Loughery. There was a new assistant coach, Rod Thorn. There was a new superstar on the horizon, Julius Erving, acquired from Virginia in an expensive but worthwhile deal. There were four newcomers fresh off collegiate campuses—Larry Kenon, John Williamson, Billy Schaeffer and Jim O'Brien. And there was another addition, Willie Sojourner, also from Virginia.

There also was a great deal of hope because there was a great deal of talent.

But in the beginning, there was a great deal of confusion, adjustments to be made, and problems to be solved.

Then Loughery began to make some changes. He scrapped his pressing defense in favor of a more sloughing one, which at times resembled an illegal zone, but concentrated on stopping the opposition's big scorers. He also scrapped his yelling and screaming tactics from the bench, efforts that often resulted in unnecessary technical fouls and resentment from his players, for a calmer attitude, but one that still was forceful and gained respect. And he made a bold move by benching the popular but slow-moving veteran Bill Melchionni, the league leader in assists each of the previous three seasons, in favor of the aggressive and cocky Williamson.

All those changes seemed to work perfectly. From

last place, the Nets, helped by a nine-game winning streak which negated the earlier losing skein, began to rise quickly from the depths. They passed the Memphis Tams, then the Virginia Squires, then the Carolina Cougars and finally the Kentucky Colonels, and in late December, they surged into first place.

They exchanged the lead with the Colonels for a while, before swinging a deal that provided them with the extra bench depth they needed—and, surprisingly, the trade was with their closest pursuer, Kentucky. They sent streak-shooting backcourtman John Roche, a player long coveted by Kentucky, to the Colonels for Wendell Ladner, an enforcer-type forward, and Mike Gale, a steadying influence at guard.

At the same time, there was a lot of wheeling and dealing around the entire league as all the teams tried to shore up for the stretch run. Kentucky, in addition to acquiring Roche from the Nets, got Red Robbins and Chuck Williams from San Diego for Jimmy O'Brien, signed Jim Bradley from Northern Illinois, sold Rick Mount to Utah and obtained Joe Hamilton from San Antonio.

Utah, battling Indiana and San Antonio for the West lead, also received Johnny Neumann from Memphis for Glen Combs, Mike Jackson and Ronnie Robinson. Indiana picked up John Baum from Memphis and Bob Netolicky from San Antonio, and signed Kevin Joyce of South Carolina. San Antonio, having purchased center Swen Nater from Virginia earlier for an estimated $300,000, then paid the poor, struggling Squires about $250,000 for George Gervin. And San Diego fortified itself by signing a pair of National Basketball Association discards, Travis Grant and Flynn Robinson.

When all the shuffling ended, it appeared that New York and Kentucky were the strongest teams in the

East, and Utah, Indiana and San Antonio the best in the West. And that's exactly the way it turned out.

The youthful Nets, despite their inexperience, held off the Colonels and won their first East championship with a 55-29 record, their best in history, and two games better than Kentucky.

Carolina, hampered by the loss of ailing Billy Cunningham, the Most Valuable Player Award winner during the 1972-73 season who underwent two kidney operations, finished third, eight games back. And Virginia, despite the loss of Nater and Gervin, managed to wind up fourth, ahead of Charles O. Finley's ragtag Tams, who set a league record for the most defeats, 63.

Utah, on the strength of a brilliant 14-game mid-season winning streak and the best home court record in the league, 33-9, won the West by five games over Indiana, with the Pacers hanging on to edge upstart San Antonio for second place by one game.

Denver and San Diego finished in a tie for fourth place; then the Conquistadors routed the Rockets 131-111 in a playoff game for the final playoff spot, giving Wilt Chamberlain some satisfaction in his first season as coach, following his many losses in court in efforts to become an active player.

Erving, the sensational Dr. J., became the league's first player to win the scoring title twice in a row, averaging 27.4 points per game. He also was named the ABA's Most Valuable Player and a member of the league's All-Star team, along with forward George McGinnis of Indiana, center Artis Gilmore of Kentucky, and guards Jimmy Jones of Utah and Mack Calvin of Carolina.

Nater edged rival center Caldwell Jones of San Diego, and Kenon for the Rookie of the Year Award, while Utah's Joe Mullaney and Kentucky's Babe McCarthy surprisingly were the co-winners of the

Coach of the Year title, ahead of Loughery and San Antonio's Tom Nissalke, who guided the Spurs to a 45-39 record after the team had been 28-56 the previous season when they were the Dallas Chaparrals.

There were other notable developments during the season, such as: new Commissioner Mike Storen showing a lot of clout in his first year on the job; the experiment with the controversial and revolutionary no-foul-out rule; the signing of a new three-year contract between the owners and players on the opening day of the season, avoiding a strike; the boycott of the All-Star Game luncheon by 10 black players; a $300,000,000 antitrust, breach of contract and fraud suit filed against the NBA; the financial instability of several clubs, including Memphis, Virginia, San Diego, Carolina and Utah, and the rejection by San Diego voters for the building of a new arena to replace the bandbox, 3,200-seat Community Concourse used as a home court by the Conquistadors.

Then came the playoffs, the so-called "second season."

In the East, the opening two rounds lasted only a total of 13 games, compared to 20 in the West.

The Nets, led by the irrepressible Erving, eliminated Virginia, his former team, in five games, and Kentucky, with the 7-foot-2 Gilmore dominating both the scoring and rebounding, kayoed injury-plagued Carolina in four straight games in the East's first round. Then the Nets, spurred by the stalwart defensive work of 25-year-old Billy Paultz, their oldest starter, against the elongated Gilmore, stunned Kentucky in the East final, ousting the disappointed, disgruntled and cold-shooting Colonels in four consecutive games.

Meanwhile, in the West, Utah was extended to six games before beating stubborn San Diego, and Indiana needed a second-half rally in the final game to overtake

San Antonio and get past the Spurs in seven games in the opening round. Then the Stars shocked the Pacers, defending league champions, by winning the first three games of their final series, but Utah lost veteran center Zelmo Beaty for the fourth game because of a severe groin infection and a 105-degree temperature, and the series turned around. The suddenly revived Pacers swept the next three games, and threatened to become the first team in pro basketball history to overcome a 3-0 playoff deficit and win a series. But the Stars choked off their bid, racing to a 109-87 victory in the final game.

And so the stage was set for the championship series ... the precocious Nets, the league's least experienced team, averaging 2.7 years of ABA experience, against the veteran, cagey Stars, the league's most experienced team, averaging 5.3 years.

The Nets, because of their better regular-season record, had the home court advantage and opened the series at the Nassau Coliseum in Uniondale, New York, where they had beaten the Stars four times without a loss during the season.

They extended that string to five, winning the opener 89-85 as Erving, with a dazzling variety of shots, scorched the nets for 47 points, his season's high. Then the Nets made it six in a row, trouncing the Stars 118-94 in a fight-punctuated second game.

The fisticuffs erupted in the opening minute, when Utah's Ron Boone punched Brian Taylor in the jaw, knocking out two teeth. But the blow later proved damaging to Boone. He suffered a hand infection, needed a lancing the following day and was forced to wear a protective bandage around the injury for game three, curtailing his shooting and ballhandling efficiency. The Stars also suffered two other injuries in the second game. Forward George Govan, who had been filling in for Beaty at center, pulled a knee ligament, and Mount was slowed by a calf injury when he collided with the rampaging Ladner.

But Beaty was back and the Stars were home, and that combination appeared to spark Utah. The Stars fought back from a 15-point, third-quarter deficit and led 94-91 until Taylor gained sweet revenge, hitting a three-point field goal at the final buzzer, tying the score and sending the game into overtime. And for the third straight time, the Nets prevailed, winning 103-100. That put them on the brink of becoming the first ABA team to sweep a final series.

But it wasn't to happen. The Stars, with Beaty scoring 18 points in the second half after going scoreless in the first two periods, outgunned New York 97-89 in game four.

That sent the series back to New York, where a capacity crowd of 15,934 sat patiently through 43½ minutes of close, tense basketball. Then, with 4½ minutes remaining, the Nets exploded, outscoring the weary but game Stars 17-5 and sweeping to a 111-100 triumph for their first ABA championship. It touched off a wild celebration. Fans stampeded out of their seats, mobbing their heroes and shattering one of the $400 glass backboards at the Coliseum. When the players finally escaped the clutches of their wild fans, they unleashed their own emotions, yelping gleefully, tossing champagne around the locker room, throwing club officials and media people into the showers, and drinking merrily.

"It's a beautiful feeling," chirped the usually subdued Taylor. "We've come a long way, a long way from adversity when we started out with a 4-10 record, and lost nine straight. It's nice to end it this way."

"They got what they deserved," said the chipper Loughery, his body soaked with champagne and water.

"Going into the playoffs, everyone wanted to play us. They felt our inexperience would hurt us. We showed them, didn't we?"

They sure did.

ABA ALL-STAR GAME

The largest crowd ever to watch a basketball game in Virginia saw the American Basketball Association's East All Stars defeat the West 128-112 in the annual mid-season game.

The game attracted a capacity 10,624 to Norfolk's Scope Arena and, ironically, the high scorer was rookie Swen Nater, who dropped in 29 points and grabbed 22 rebounds for the West. Nater had been sold by Virginia to San Antonio earlier in the season and every time he scored a basket or grabbed a rebound, the home fans hooted Squires' owner Earl Foreman, who had dealt him away.

The East's best scorer was Dan Issel of Kentucky, who had 21 points. Teammate Artis Gilmore was the game's most valuable player with 18 points, 13 rebounds and four blocked shots.

In the first period, the East opened a 10-point lead and maintained that margin most of the way. The West's Ron Boone scored the game's lone three-point play.

The box score:

WEST (112): Wise 4 0-0 8; McGinnis 7 0-0 14; Daniels 2 1-2 5; Jones 4 3-5 11; Jabali 3 0-1 6; Johnson 3 2-2 8; R. Jones 2 0-0 4; Nater 13 3-4 29; Boone 7 0-0 15; Simpson 6 0-0 12; Totals 51 9-14.

EAST (128): Erving 6 2-2 14; Issel 10 1-1 21; Gilmore 8 2-3 18; Dampier 8 0-0 16; Calvin 3 2-3 8; Gervin 3 3-4 9; Kenon 8 2-3 18; Eakins 1 0-0 2;

McClain 6 0-0 12; Thompson 5 0-0 10; Totals 58 12-16.

West	25	30	29	28	—112
East	35	27	37	29	—128

Three-point field goals—Boone.
Fouled Out—None.
Total Fouls—West 18; East 18.
Attendance—10,624.

ABM MVP—ERVING

Julius Erving, called the most exciting player in pro basketball after his sensational play led the New York Nets to their finest season, was named the Most Valuable Player in the American Basketball Association for 1973-74.

The 24-year-old superstar compiled 49 votes of sportswriters and sportscasters in the league's 10 cities as he easily outdistanced Artis Gilmore of Kentucky, who was named on nine ballots. None of the other six players listed received more than two votes.

Erving, a 6-7 third year forward who simply dumbfounds fans and players alike with moves never before seen on the basketball court, became the first player to win two consecutive ABA scoring championships, averaging 27.4 points a game.

But that is only part of the story, part of the method in which Dr. J operated this season. He also finished seventh in the league in rebounding with 10.7 a game; ninth in two-point field goal accuracy, 51.5%; sixth in assists, 5.2; third in blocked shots, 204, and third in steals, 190.

He also hit 39.5%; from three-point range, high enough to win that statistical title if he had shot enough to qualify. His free throw percentage was a respectable 76.6%; and he was behind only Gilmore in minutes played this season with 3,398 as he played in all 84 games.

Those statistics helped the Nets to the best record in their seven-year history, 55-29, and their first Eastern Division crown. Erving's spectacular play also made him and the Nets one of the top attractions in the league at the gate.

Gilmore, the 7-2 dominating pivot man for the second place Colonels in the East, won this honor in his rookie season in 1972. He was the league's leading rebounder for the third consecutive season with 18.3 a game and ranked 11th in scoring with 18.7 points per contest. He also had the second most blocked shots, 287.

Billy Cunningham of Carolina won the MVP award last season, but was out most of this year with a kidney ailment. Other previous winners were Connie Hawkins of Pittsburgh in 1968, Mel Daniels of Indiana in 1969, Spencer Haywood in 1970 and Daniels again in 1971.

Erving, a native of Roosevelt, New York, only a short distance from the Nets' Nassau Coliseum home, joined the Nets this season after playing two years with the Virginia Squires.

Averaging 27.3 points a game and then 31.9, he was named second team All League in his rookie year and then first team last season. He also was selected to the first team All Rookie squad, losing out to Gilmore as Rookie of the Year.

After twice leading the Squires into the playoffs, Erving signed a future contract with Atlanta of the National Basketball Association for the 1975-76 season. That prompted his trade to the Nets on August 1, 1973, for a large sum of money. The Nets also settled any claim that Atlanta had to Erving by paying the Hawks another undisclosed amount of cash.

Erving then signed a new eight-year contract with the Nets at an amount to be well into six figures.

ABA ALL-LEAGUE TEAM

Julius Erving of the New York Nets, named the league's Most Valuable Player, also led the voting for the American Basketball Association's 1973-74 All League Team.

Dr. J., 6-7 forward who was the first player to win two consecutive ABA scoring titles, polled 132 points on 66 first team votes of sportswriters and sportscasters in the 10 league cities. He was mentioned on every ballot.

Artis Gilmore of the Kentucky Colonels was selected the first team center for the third straight season. He was named first on 61 ballots and totaled 125 points.

James Jones of the Utah Stars was the top vote-getter in the backcourt, polling 113 points with 54 first team votes as he made the top squad for the third time and second time in a row.

At the other forward was Indiana's George McGinnis with 34 top votes and 98 points, with Mack Calvin of Carolina at the other guard with 28 first team votes and 77 points.

On the second team were center Swen Nater of San Antonio (22), forwards Dan Issel of Kentucky (80) and Willie Wise of Utah (61) and guards Ron Boone of Utah (48) and Louie Dampier of Kentucky (42).

Erving, who averaged 27.4 points a game and ranked in the top 10 in five other statistical categories as he led the Eastern Division Nets to the top record in the league, made the first team for the second successive season after being named to the second five his first year in the league. He averaged 10.7 rebounds, hit 51.5%; from the field, had 5.2 assists a game and ranked third in blocked shots and steals with 204 and 190, respectively.

Gilmore, 7-2, who has led the league in rebounding all three of his seasons—18.3 a game this year—in the ABA while also scoring 18.2 points a game, was the top center selection for the third year in a row. He also blocked 287 shots to rank second in the league.

Jones, 6-4, an original player in the league, scored 16.8 points a game, ranked second in field goal percentage at 55.1%; led the league in free throw shooting at 88.4%; and tied Erving for fifth in assists with 5.2 a game as he helped the Stars to the Western Division crown.

McGinnis, a 6-8 third year player who mixes overwhelming strength with agility, ranked second in both scoring and rebounding with 25.89 points and 14.95 rebounds per contest. He also was sixth in steals with 159 as he moved up from last year's second squad.

Calvin, the smallest man on the squad at 6-0 but with extraordinary quickness, also made the second five last season after making the first team in 1971. Taking over more of the scoring load after Billy Cunningham was disabled, Calvin averaged 18 points a game, tied Boone for second in free throw shooting at 87.5%, and was 10th in steals with 135.

ABA CO-COACHES OF YEAR
MULLANEY AND McCARTHY

Joe Mullaney and Babe McCarthy, two veteran coaches long overlooked by voters, were selected co-Coaches of the Year in the American Basketball Association.

Mullaney, the coach of the Utah Stars, and McCar-

thy of the Kentucky Colonels tied for the honor in the
voting of ABA coaches. It was the second time in the
league's seven-year history that there was a deadlock.
Bill Sharman and Joe Belmont tied in 1970.

Mullaney, who came to Utah after guiding Kentucky
to the seventh game of the championship series last season before losing, took the Stars to a runaway Western
Division title.

McCarthy, nicknamed Magnolia Mouth for his
Southern accent and outgoing manner, guided a re-
vamped Kentucky team through a torrid fight with New
York for first place in the Eastern Division, a race that
went to the final two days of the season.

In three seasons, Mullaney, a former successful
coach at Providence College, has become one of the
winningest coaches in the ABA after his Kentucky
team won a record 68 games in 1971-72 and then won
56 last season, finishing second in the East by one
game.

During his first two seasons as a professional coach,
he won 46 and 48 games at Los Angeles in the National Basketball Association, finishing second and first
in the division and going to the seventh game of the
title series before losing in the first year.

Mullaney had an overall record of 218-114 entering
this season with a 29-26 playoff record. His record in
the ABA was a glittering 124-44 for a .738 percentage.

After a slow start this season, Mullaney's Utah team
ran off 14 straight victories to pull far ahead in the
West as they overcame injuries and adjusted to several
changes in personnel through trades during the season.

McCarthy, who had been coaching in the ABA since
the first year except for the final two weeks of last season, won the West title with New Orleans the first year
of the league. That team went to the final game of the
championship series before losing to Pittsburgh.

McCarthy's team finished second the next year and then fifth despite a .500 record. Given little material the last three seasons at Memphis and then Dallas, McCarthy's team did not fare well.

This season, Kentucky was near the top all year despite changes that brought no less than six new players acquired by them through trades during the season. However, at season's end McCarthy was dismissed by the Colonel's management.

Previous winners of the award were Vince Cazetta of Pittsburgh in 1968, Alex Hannum of Oakland in 1969, Sharman and Belmont in 1970, Al Bianchi of Virginia in 1971, Tom Nissalke of Dallas in 1972 and Larry Brown of Carolina last season.

ABA ROOKIE OF THE YEAR AND ALL ROOKIE TEAM

Swen Nater of the San Antonio Spurs, who did not start playing basketball until he entered college and then sat two years in Bill Walton's shadow, was named Rookie of the Year in the American Basketball Association.

The rawboned 6-11 native of Holland barely edged another 6-11 center, Caldwell Jones of the San Diego Conquistadors, in the balloting of sportswriters and sportscasters in the 10 league cities. The vote was 24-23.

Larry Kenon, another big man who started all season for the New York Nets, was third with 14 votes. His teammate, John Williamson, a 6-2 guard, received three.

Nater beat out Jones for the center spot on the All Rookie team, 88-78, with two points going for the first team vote and one for second team. Kenon was the top vote getter on the squad with 126.

Dwight Lamar, the flashy first year hotshot with San Diego, compiled 123 points to team in the backcourt with Williamson, who had 104 points. The other forward was Mike Green, a 6-10 stringbean with Denver, who had 50 points.

Joining Jones on the second team were forwards Tim Bassett of San Diego, and Jim Bradley of Kentucky and guards Bird Averitt and George Karl, both of San Antonio.

San Antonio and San Diego thus landed three players each on the two teams in the balanced voting in which 20 rookies were named on at least one ballot.

Nater follows New York's Brian Taylor, who was the top rookie last season. Other winners were Mel Daniels in 1968, Warren Armstrong (Jabali) in 1969, Spencer Haywood in 1970, Dan Issel and Charlie Scott (tie) in 1971 and Artis Gilmore in 1972.

Nater, a rugged 250 pounder who started the season with Virginia and then was traded to San Antonio for a reported $300,000 and a high draft choice on November 21, was the fourth leading rebounder in the league with 12.6 a game and won the two-point field goal shooting crown at 55.3%.

He averaged 12.6 points a game as a reserve in 17 games with Virginia and then jumped to 14.5 when he stepped into San Antonio's starting lineup, for an overall total of 14.1.

Nater did not move to the United States until he was nine years old and did not start playing basketball until he enrolled at Cyprus Junior College.

By his second season, he averaged 23 points and 18 rebounds a game, enough to impress John Wooden at UCLA.

However, at UCLA, he sat on the bench two seasons behind the great Walton. He did not move into the spotlight until the series between the United States and Russia in the summer of 1973.

Virginia, which gained the rights to Nater in the 1972 dispersal draft, out-bid Milwaukee of the National Basketball Association, which drafted him in the first round.

In camp, he immediately caught the eye of Coach Al Bianchi, although Nater himself admits, "I'm still not caught up with guys who have been playing all their lives."

In the ABA All Star game in January, Nater poured in 29 points and grabbed 22 rebounds.

Jones, a little known performer from Albany, Station Georgia, who followed brother Wilbert of the Memphis Tams into the ABA, led the league in blocked shots with 316. Drafted in the third round by Virginia, he finished 22nd in scoring with 15 points a game and third in rebounding with 13.9 after San Diego acquired the rights to him.

Kenon, a 6-9 forward from 1973 NCAA-runnerup Memphis State, ranked 17th in scoring with 15.9 points a game and sixth in rebounding with 11.5. Williamson, an unheralded guard from New Mexico State, averaged 14.5 points a game after winning a starting berth from All Star Bill Melchionni early in the season.

Lamar, 6-1, of Southwestern Louisiana, averaged 20.4 points and Green, of Louisiana Tech, averaged 11.4 points and 7.4 rebounds. Bassett, 6-8, of Georgia, averaged 6.9 points and 7.3 rebounds; Bradley, 6-8, from Northern Illinois, 8.3 points and 6.1 rebounds; Averitt, 6-2, from Pepperdine, 11.5 points and Karl, 6-2, from North Carolina, 7.8 points.

THE SEASON PRESENT

NBA Present

"We're No. 1," yelled a crowd of hardy Boston fans who had braved a torrential rainstorm to welcome home their Celtic heroes after the team had won the 1974 National Basketball Association championship, beating the Bucks in the seventh game of the final series at Milwaukee.

Indeed, the Celtics were No. 1. For the first time in five years, and for the first time without Bill Russell, they were NBA champions.

With Russell at center, they had won 11 league titles in 13 years, from 1957 to 1969. Without him, they had won none—until they outlasted the Bucks.

"This team has a lot of pride," said John Havlicek, the Celtics' captain and the Most Valuable Player in the grueling championship series. "The younger players don't want to hear about the old Celtics any more. They want to prove they have championship quality themselves."

They did. And now they want to do it again, to show their consistency, the mark of a champion.

"The first championships were all the old Celtic tradition," added Havlicek. "But this is the start of a new tradition."

It no longer is the era of Russell, Bob Cousy, Bill Sharman, Sam Jones, K.C. Jones, Tom Heinsohn and Frank Ramsey. It is the era of Havlicek, Dave Cowens, Jo Jo White, Don Chaney, Don Nelson, Paul Silas and Paul Westphal.

Now the Celtics are going to have to make room for another championship flag in Boston Garden. For home games, they turn the arena into a private Hall of Flags. Hanging from the rafters are all the championship flags and banners bearing the retired numbers of some of their former great players.

But this is a new era and a virtually new team, with pride, determination and confidence. It is a team with incredible durability, stamina, speed, hustle, tenacity and mobility. It may not be the most talented club in the league, but it makes the most of what it has.

"When we had Russell," said Havlicek, "we just expected to win it [the title] all the time. Last season took us four years. This team is young and it realizes these opportunities don't come around that often."

How true. There are several teams in the league, including the Buffalo Braves, the Portland Trail Blazers, the Detroit Pistons and the Washington Bullets who are rapidly building toward championship caliber. And Milwaukee, the New York Knicks, Chicago Bulls and Los Angeles Lakers could dethrone the Celtics this season.

In the Atlantic Division, the Celtics—with their racehorse offense and pressing, trapping defense—will get their strongest challenges in quest of their fourth straight title from the youthful Braves and the veteran Knicks.

Buffalo carried Boston to six games before losing to the Celtics in a bitterly contested opening-round playoff series last season after finishing with its first over-.500 record in its four-year history. The Braves have one of the smartest general managers in the league in Eddie Donovan, who with clever trades and draft picks has built the Braves into bona-fide contenders.

The club is built around Bob McAdoo, the 1973-74 scoring champion, and little Ernie DiGregorio, the fancy playmaker and league leader in assists last season as a rookie. There is also a strong supporting cast, with Jim McMillian, Garfield Heard, Jack Marin, Randy Smith, Matt Guokas and perhaps No. 1 draft choice Tom McMillen, the Rhodes Scholarship winner from Maryland.

The Knicks, NBA champions in 1970 and 1973, have a large rebuilding job following the losses of Dave DeBusschere, Jerry Lucas and Dean Meminger. DeBusschere, the brawny forward and heart of the club, retired to become general manager of the champion New York Nets of the American Basketball Association. Lucas retired after becoming discouraged over his lack of playing time last season, and Meminger was lost in the expansion draft for the new New Orleans franchise and wound up at Atlanta.

To replace them, the Knicks acquired sharpshooting forward Howard Porter plus a 1975 second-round draft choice from Chicago for their 1974 No. 1 draft selection, drafted highly regarded collegians Jesse Dark of Virginia Commonwealth and Rudy Jackson of Hutchinson (Kansas) Junior College and gave a tryout to former ABA All-Star guard Warren Jabali.

They still have Walt Frazier and Earl Monroe, one of the most productive backcourt combinations in the league.

Philadelphia, slowly returning to respectability, figured to improve even more with the addition of muscular Marvin Barnes, their No. 1 draft pick from Providence College. Barnes was an All-American last season after leading the nation in rebounding. The 76ers also were hopeful of regaining the services of their former All-Star forward, Billy Cunningham, who jumped to the ABA two years ago, and were counting on other draftees such as Don Smith of Dayton and Coniel Norman of Arizona to add scoring punch and defense.

They also were hoping to get a full season out of Doug Collins, their No. 1 draft choice last season, who played only 25 games because of injuries. And they still had Fred Carter and Tom Van Arsdale, two 20-points-per-game scorers.

In the Central Division, it doesn't seem to make any difference what first name they apply to the Bullets—whether it's Baltimore, Capital or Washington—the team keeps winning the title. And there is no indication to believe otherwise this season.

The Bullets, provided they can keep center Wes Unseld and guard Archie Clark healthy, should have a team with great depth for the first time in years. Behind the front line of Unseld, Clark, rebounding champion Elvin Hayes, Mike Riordan and Phil Chenier, there will be slick Kevin Porter, Nick Weatherspoon and their two top draftees, Leonard Robinson of Tennessee State and Dennis DuVal of Syracuse.

Atlanta, which finished last season as a disorganized, disenchanted and disgruntled club, quickly set out to regroup by dealing controversial Pete Maravich, the league's second leading scorer, to New Orleans. In return, the Hawks received a bundle of draft choices, including New Orleans' first guard and first forward in the expansion pool. They turned out to be Meminger and Bob Kauffman.

In addition, they had two picks in the first round of the regular draft and took two impressive youngsters, Tom Henderson, the slick ball-handler, playmaker and shooter from Hawaii, and Mike Sojourner of Utah, the Most Valuable Player in last season's National Invitation Tournament.

Maravich's departure prompted Coach Cotton Fitzsimmons to move All-Star forward Lou Hudson back to guard, his more natural position; and the loss of veteran center Walt Bellamy to New Orleans in the expansion draft enabled the Hawks to go with either Dwight Jones, a rookie last season, or Sojourner at center.

Houston, a high-scoring club led by Rudy Tomjanovich, diminutive Calvin Murphy and Mike Newlin, lacked offensive power at center and hoped it was found in the draft with the selection of Bobby Jones of North Carolina.

Cleveland also needed the important big man in the middle and the Cavaliers went out and got him, obtaining 6-11 Jim Chones from the Los Angeles Lakers for a No. 1 1975 draft choice. Chones actually played with the Carolina Cougars of the ABA last season, averaging better than 14 points per game. But he averaged only half as many rebounds and his attitude was questionable, so the Cougars cut him after the season. Since his NBA rights belonged to Los Angeles, the Cavaliers had to deal with the Lakers.

The Cavaliers also found themselves short of a proven guard alongside All-Star Austin Carr when veteran Len Wilkens retired as a player and took the coaching job with Portland. But again they went into the trade market, acquiring Dick Snyder in exchange for 1974 and future draft choices.

Cleveland also made an impressive draft pick, taking high-scoring Campy Russell of Michigan.

New Orleans, hoping to be successful in an area in which the ABA previously failed, made a smart move in getting Maravich, a former star at Louisiana State University, from the Hawks as a drawing card in its first season of operation. It also was a costly move, as New Orleans traded a good deal of its future in draft picks.

Then, by dipping into the usually thin expansion pool, New Orleans drafted such players as Stu Lantz, Curtis Perry, Jim Barnett, Bellamy, Steve Kuberski,

Dennis Awtrey, John Block and Bud Stallworth. Of that group, most of whom have been starters in the league, New Orleans should glean a respectable if not yet highly competitive club.

New Orleans' new coach, Scotty Robertson, is another local product, having been lured from Louisiana Tech, and the club will have the distinction of being the first basketball team to play in the new Superdome.

The Midwest Division was the most highly competitive last season and figures to be again this season, with the same three contenders—Milwaukee, Chicago and Detroit—vying for the title.

The Bucks, with the most dominating giant in the game, Kareem Abdul-Jabbar, three-time Most Valuable Player in his five years as a pro, again have to be rated favorites. But Milwaukee still is continuing its long search for a power forward to complement slender Bob Dandridge.

In the backcourt, they will welcome the return of Lucius Allen, sidelined for the entire playoffs last season after undergoing knee surgery, and hope that aging Oscar Robertson does not wear out too quickly. Most likely, Coach Larry Costello will rest Robertson a great deal and look for more production from Jon McGlocklin, Ron Williams and rookie Gary Brokaw from Notre Dame.

Chicago, perennial runner-up to Milwaukee, had an extremely difficult job of holding off Detroit for second place last season. And if the Bulls don't find a high-scoring center, which they have lacked for years, it may be even tougher this season.

Forwards Bob Love and Chet Walker likely will provide the bulk of the scoring again, but should have help up front from rookies Maurice Lucas, a junior from Marquette, and Clifton Pondexter, a freshman from Long Beach State. The backcourt also is solid, with Norm Van Lier, Jerry Sloan and Bob Weiss.

Detroit, coming off its winningest season in history and its first playoff berth in six years, has two of the finest shooters in the league in burly center Bob Lanier and steady guard Dave Bing. But the key to the Pistons' success last season was that Coach of the Year Ray Scott taught his club to play team ball in the style that carried the Knicks to their two recent championships. If the Pistons can continue that pattern, they should make a strong challenge for the title.

Kansas City-Omaha, like New Orleans, will be playing on a new court this season, the Crosby Kemper Memorial Arena in Kansas City, where 30 of its 41 home games are scheduled. And like New Orleans, the Kings may have trouble winning, unless little Nate Archibald regains his form of two seasons ago, when he was the league's scoring champion and assist leader.

Archibald was crippled by an Achilles tendon injury last season and appeared in only 35 games. If he has fully recuperated, he could form one of the NBA's most devastating backcourts, along with Jimmy Walker.

The Kings need help up front, however, and hope to get it from draftees Scott Wedman from Colorado and Lloyd Batts from Cincinnati.

The Pacific Division appears the most unpredictable and possibly the most interesting of the league's four sections. What makes it so intriguing is the presence of Bill Walton, the three-time All-American and two-time Player of the Year, on Portland, the team that finished last in the division during the 1973-74 season.

Thus, Walton's ability to turn around a franchise—like Jabbar did with Milwaukee upon joining the team in 1969—will be tested immediately. So will his tender knees. Will they be able to stand the grind of an 82-game schedule?

Walton joins a team that already includes two All-Stars, forward Sidney Wicks and guard Geoff Petrie, but lacks another strong forward and guard. However, his presence, if he plays to his potential, could inspire his teammates to perform beyond their capabilities and lift the Trail Blazers to the title.

The Trail Blazers also have a new coach in Wilkens. He replaces Jack McCloskey, who resigned, citing irreconcilable differences with management.

Los Angeles is the defending division champion, having overtaken Golden State in the final week of the season, but both California teams are questionable entering the 1974-75 season. The Lakers' biggest question mark revolves around the availability of perennial All-Star guard Jerry West, sidelined with an abdominal injury most of last season. Without West, the Lakers lack leadership. But they still have streak-shooting Gail Goodrich, promising Jim Price, shot-blocking center Elmore Smith, erratic Connie Hawkins and veteran rebounders Happy Hairston and Bill Bridges.

Golden State needs help quickly. Two of the Warriors' long-time stars, Nate Thurmond and Jeff Mullins, are going downhill rapidly, and they lost Jim Barnett in the expansion draft. Also, 20-point scorer Cazzie Russell played out his option and said he would not sign with the club again.

All-NBA forward Rick Barry appeared to be the team's only player still with a strong rating. A newcomer who could help is All-American forward Keith Wilkes of UCLA.

Seattle, which made tremendous strides late last season under the coaching guidance of Bill Russell, was banking on the league's tallest player, 7-4 rookie Tom Burleson from North Carolina State, to continue its climb upward.

The SuperSonics again will be paced by superstar

forward Spencer Haywood, and a potential superstar, Fred Brown, in the backcourt. But the loss of Snyder will hurt.

Phoenix fell apart last season after scoring leader Charlie Scott suffered a double compound fracture of his left arm, just past the half way point of the campaign. But with Scott back and the addition of rookie All-American John Shumate from Notre Dame, the Suns hope to shine this season.

ABA Present

The youthful New York Nets, champions of the American Basketball Association for the first time, already are being hailed as the next sports dynasty, but superstar Julius Erving is both cautious and optimistic in assessing the team's chances for continued success.

"It's all in front of us," he said in thinking about the possibility of the Nets repeating as champions in the 1974-75 season and blitzing the league the way they did last season.

Then he warned, "Everyone is talking about us building a dynasty in the '70s, but I think it's improbable. Things are different these days.

"Basketball is the sport of the '70s and there are just too many good ballplayers coming out of college these days for one team to dominate. Players are better now and the talent is spread around.

"The teams that had dynasties were able to maintain them because they got the talent together and blended it," he continued. "But now, with so much talent around, the poorer teams get better. That's what happened to Indiana [the 1973 ABA champion] last season. They weren't able to keep up with the other clubs."

It doesn't figure to happen to the Nets this season.

With their youth, exuberance, confidence and, most important of all, talent—particularly the incredible Erving—they could rule the league for many years.

But again, Erving emphasized the Nets would be hard-pressed to maintain their supremacy this season. "I don't think we'll be complacent," he predicted. "We have so many points to improve on. We lost nine in a row at one time [last season] and we don't want that to happen again. We shouldn't lose more than two in a row this season before we're able to regroup.

"We will be under pressure to play well consistently," he added. "Consistency is what separates the bad teams from the good and the good ones from the great ones. The emphasis should be on getting prepared for every game. Then you stand a chance of winning—a good chance."

With Erving, the league's Most Valuable Player last season and the scoring champion for the second year in a row—and rapidly gaining acclaim as the best all-around player in basketball—the Nets stand an excellent chance of defending their Eastern Division title and sweeping to the league title again.

"Dr. J. gives us the feeling we can't lose . . . that if we keep it close, the Doctor will come through and do his thing," said starting guard Brian Taylor.

"Erving makes the job enjoyable," said the Nets' colorful coach, Kevin Loughery, who replaced Lou Carnesecca last season. "I have never seen anyone play better. When he makes a move and doesn't score, I'm really surprised. I expect him to score every time he gets the ball."

But the Nets' success is not due to Erving alone. They have two starters who actually should be beginning their first years of pro ball, but who were first-stringers last season. They are kangaroo-like forward Larry Kenon and guard John Williamson, the self-pro-claimed "Super John," both of whom left college one year early to join the ABA. The Nets' center is underrated Billy Paultz, and there is a solid bench, including forwards Wendell Ladner, Billy Schaeffer and Jim O'Brien, pivotman Willie Sojourner and guards Mike Gale and Bill Melchionni.

Defensively, the Nets play a trapping, pressure defense which greatly impresses Memphis Coach Bill van Breda Kolff. "Defense starts with two guards, and both Williamson and Taylor are quick and have great court sense," observed van Breda Kolff. "And if their men get by them, the Nets have three guys who can block shots [a reference to Erving, Kenon and Paultz]. Those same three guys can also rebound.

"On offense, they all can score, are good with the ball off the break and can finish a play. If they don't get a layup on the break, they're all capable of stopping short and hitting the jumper.

"They've got a fantastic team."

Alex Hannum, the deposed coach and general manager of the Denver Rockets, agreed. "You would have to take a hard look to find a better basketball team in the country right now than the Nets," said Hannum.

The rest of the ABA teams would have to concur with that observation.

This season, the Nets will have another great player in their midst, but he won't be on the court. Dave DeBusschere, the former National Basketball Association All-Star forward with the New York Knicks, and now the Nets' general manager, is under a 10-year Nets' contract for $750,000.

The final words on the chances of a Nets' dynasty belong to Coach Loughery. "We have a young team and if we can keep the nucleus, this could develop into quite a ball club."

It is quite a club already, as the other ABA clubs

found out last season and will realize again this season.

Not only were the Nets the most artistic club in the league in 1973-74, they were the most successful financially at the gate, averaging 8,923 fans per game, the best figure in the league.

Only three other franchises were solid and assured of showing up in the standings this season. They were Kentucky, runner-up to the Nets in the East during the regular season and playoffs—and in attendance, with an average of 8,190; Indiana, third in attendance with a 7,577 average, and San Antonio, fifth with 6,232.

The Utah Stars, Western Division champions and losers to the Nets in the championship series, finished fourth in attendance at 6,877. But the Stars were shaky, because owner Bill Daniels was attempting to sell the club and thinking of purchasing the Denver team. Denver is his hometown.

Denver owners Frank Goldberg and Bud Fischer are from San Diego, and after unceremoniously dumping Alex Hannum as coach and general manager following a disastrous season in which the Rockets failed to make the playoffs, were seeking to purchase the Conquistadors.

The possibilities for a game of ABA musical chairs appeared endless. Tedd Munchak said he wanted to remain in business, but not in Carolina, and closed up all three Cougars' offices after the team failed in a quiet but concerted bid to land UCLA All-American Bill Walton. Before closing up shop, Munchak cut center Jim Chones, who still had four years remaining on his contract, and sold Ted McClain, one of the league's best defensive guards, to Kentucky. He also gave permission to Coach Larry Brown, general manager Carl Scheer and All-Star guard Mack Calvin to negotiate with Denver.

The other three franchises—San Diego, Memphis and Virginia—also were shaky.

Dr. Leonard Bloom, San Diego's owner, was told by ABA Commissioner Mike Storen to find a bigger arena than the 3,200-seat Community Concourse the Conquistadors used last season, or move the franchise to another city, such as Los Angeles.

Memphis owner Charles O. Finley was trying to sell his team, hopefully to Stax Records, a large music recording company in Memphis, but there were difficulties in completing the deal. Finley finally sold the club.

And financially troubled Earl Foreman, owner of the Virginia team, also was running into snags in trying to unload his club. He, too, finally sold.

There also was another deal in the works for the sale of the Utah team, but that fell through at the last minute.

Furthermore, there was the uncertainty of a national television package. A deal last season with the Hughes Sports Network was a flop. Very few market areas were cleared for the ABA's All-Star Game or its late playoff games, and the final game of the championship series between New York and Utah wasn't even shown on the network, because the major market area, New York, would have been blacked out.

Through all the uncertainty and confusion, Storen remained optimistic that the league would survive its eighth season. He even talked about expansion, mentioning Los Angeles, Chicago, Tampa and the Albany-Schenectady areas as possible sites for future franchises. And he still was sticking to his original promise of making the ABA the strongest pro basketball league in existence.

The league did indeed have some outstanding players and well-established teams, but the overall picture was bleak.

Kentucky, with 7-foot-2 Artis Gilmore, the most dominating center in the league, and rugged Dan Issel, along with a solid cast of supporting veterans, including Louie Dampier, John Roche, Chuck Williams, Walt Simon and Red Robbins, again figured to give the Nets their toughest challenge in the East.

Virginia, having sold its two best players—Swen Nater and George Gervin—to San Antonio last season for $300,000 and $250,000, respectively; Memphis, led by All-Star guard George Thompson, and Carolina with 1972-73 MVP Billy Cunningham, all were uncertain commodities.

In the West, Utah appeared the best, but their fortunes hinged on their ability to pacify veteran center Zelmo Beaty. The two parties were at odds last season after Beaty held out throughout training camp and missed the early part of the season.

Still, the Stars had one of the best backcourt combinations in the league in Jimmy Jones and Ron Boone, plus the best defensive player in the ABA in forward Willie Wise.

Indiana was counting on All-Star forward George McGinnis, whose contract expired after last season, aging center Mel Daniels, veteran forward Roger Brown, Darnell Hillman and guards Freddie Lewis, Don Buse, Billy Keller and Kevin Joyce.

San Antonio, scheduled to host this season's All-Star game, had a standout front line in Nater, Gervin and All-Star Rich Jones and a young, improving backcourt that included James Silas, William "Bird" Averitt and George Karl.

At San Diego, Wilt Chamberlain was anxiously waiting to shed his role as only a coach and become a player-coach, joining a group of promising youngsters in Caldwell Jones, Dwight Lamar and Tim Bassett plus two sharpshooting NBA dropouts—Travis "The Machine" Grant and Flynn Robinson.

And at Denver, the Rockets were hoping to regroup under a new coach and new owners while satisfying backcourt ace Ralph Simpson, who had expressed his displeasure at playing for the team.

THE PLAYERS

KAREEM ABDUL-JABBAR

He stands under the basket, daring opponents to drive the lane, destroying layups with his awesome presence. Avoiding him on defense is like trying to drive around some kind of enormous statue under the basket. On offense, he flicks the ball almost nonchalantly, and invariably it slips cleanly through the basket. At a listed 7-feet-2-inches he is like a Milwaukee monument, planted under the Bucks' boards. He is Kareem Abdul-Jabbar, easily the most dominant player in professional basketball today.

How good is Abdul-Jabbar? One measure might involve thumbing through the rosters of every team in both major professional leagues. Pick out only the biggest and best names—Dr. J., Clyde, Cowens, Hayes, Gilmore, Barry. There isn't one of them who could be traded even-up, one-for-one, in a deal for Kareem. That's how good he is.

It has been five years since Abdul-Jabbar came into the NBA with the Milwaukee club. Overnight, he turned the Bucks from a nondescript expansion franchise into one of the league's power teams. Three times in those five seasons, including 1973-74, he was voted the most valuable player in the league. That vote is not from writers or coaches, but from the people who know Abdul-Jabbar's impact best—the opposing players.

Elmore Smith, no shrimp himself at 7-1, was asked about Abdul-Jabbar one night after the big guy had scored 39 points against the Los Angeles Lakers. He had been at his imposing best on defense and had riddled Smith with a variety of hooks, jumps and drives on offense.

"When he's like that," shrugged Smith, "there's nothing you can do, so you may as well forget it."

Cleveland's Steve Patterson spent three years at UCLA watching Abdul-Jabbar, who was called Lew Alcindor in those days. He still stands in awe of the giant. "Kareem's offensive potential is unlimited," said Patterson. "He can score 35 and not even get untracked. He scored 49 against us one game last year and didn't even break a sweat."

Abdul-Jabbar averaged 27 points per game for the Bucks last season, third best in the league. He connected on 54% of his shots, second best in the league. He was the No. 4 rebounder with an average of 14.5 recoveries per game and he blocked 283 shots, also second best in the league. Of all his statistics, the one Coach Larry Costello appreciated most was listed under games played. Kareem missed only one game all year and that was a vital factor for the injury-riddled Bucks.

"Kareem does what we ask of him," said Costello. "We have really been hard hit with injuries this year and he has taken up the slack. He only missed one game this year and we needed him to pick up some of the scoring when Oscar [Robertson] and Bob [Dandridge] were out with injuries. This year, he really didn't have a backup center for the first time because of Dick Cunningham's injury, meaning he had to play more and under more pressure."

In the midst of Milwaukee's rush to the NBA's Midwest Division title, Costello saluted his big man's durability. "He's just been great," the coach said. "I know he's tired and needs a rest, but we have no offense when he's out of there. He's not only a great player,

but he's a super person. He could make my job so
tough if he wanted to, but he never gives me any trouble at all. He never complains, does his job every night
and is the greatest person I've ever been associated with
in athletics."

Abdul-Jabbar is basically a very private person, de-
fined by reporters as a tough interview. He is not the
outgoing, quotable type of athlete such as Muhammad
Ali. Rather, he keeps his feelings to himself and zealously protects his privacy—as much privacy as a man
his size can manage. His demeanor is probably an out-
growth of the shroud of silence with which his
coaches—Jack Donohue at New York's Power Memorial High School and John Wooden at UCLA—
covered the young man.

Interviews had to be routed through his coaches and
rarely was a reporter allowed to go one-on-one with the
big guy. On the court, opponents would be foolhardy to
go one-on-one with him. In four years of high school,
his teams ran up a 95-6 record. At UCLA, he played
three varsity seasons and the Bruins' mark was 88-2.
That's eight losses in seven seasons, which explains why
Milwaukee brass celebrated madly after winning the
coin flip for No. 1 draft choice in 1969, the year
Kareem became available to the pros.

Abdul-Jabbar's ABA rights belonged to the New
York Nets and the big guy refused to be the subject of
a bidding war between the two leagues. He directed the
two teams to each submit one, sealed, unchangeable bid
for his services. There would be no auction for him.
Milwaukee won with a $1,400,000 bid and instantly
moved from last place to second place. A year later,
the Bucks won the NBA championship in only the
franchise's third season.

It was after the Bucks won the title that Abdul-Jabbar adopted his Islamic name. "It means 'Generous,'

to live up to these attributes and kind of incorpo-
'Servant of Allah,' and 'Powerful,' he explained. "I try
rate these things into my life."

Kareem became interested in the Islamic faith while
at UCLA and in his first year at Milwaukee. Once he
adopted the religion, it was no passing diversion. He
has made a deep study of it and toured the world in
quest of more information. It's a long way from the
sidewalks of New York where he grew up a gangly boy
whose primary diversions were the football Giants, the
baseball Dodgers and, naturally enough for a seven-
foot boy growing up in Manhattan, the then-hapless
basketball Knickerbockers.

"My year was 1955," he recalled with a smile. That
was the year the Dodgers won their first World Series
and every Brooklyn fan made sure the world remembered the occasion. "I was in the third grade and everybody in my school were Yankee fans. They had an
endless winter of me," he said.

"I was a diehard Giant fan in the seventh and eighth
grades. I went to all their games and sat in the bleach-
ers. That's why my number is 33. That was Mel
Triplett's number." Triplett was a Giant fullback. "I
used to buy two cups of coffee and just hold them to
keep my hands warm. I spent about a dollar on
coffee."

Then there were the basketball Knickerbockers.
"Very sad," remembered Kareem. "Charlie Tyra. Don-
nis Butcher, Cleveland Buckner."

Very sad indeed. The Knicks were a sorry collection
in those days. Ironically, around the corner from the
old Madison Square Garden, the local Catholic high
school, Power Memorial, had assembled a more exciting club than the pros down the street. The most exciting part of that team was the seven-foot center.

"I was always taller than the other kids, but I was

younger, too," said Abdul-Jabbar. "You kind of withdraw in that situation." He was playing varsity ball at the age of 14 when the rest of the team was composed of 16- and 17-year-olds, getting ready for college. He was protected like a fine work of art by his coaches and, in a way, there is the feeling that the sheltered life he led slowed the development of his personality.

When he chose UCLA from the thousands of colleges bidding for him, it was almost an instant replay for four more years with the then Lew Alcindor helping his school to victory after victory and the public learning very little about what kind of a person this giant of a man was.

Only after he got to Milwaukee, and established himself as one of the best players ever to trot on a basketball court, did he begin to shed some of his anonymity.

Who is he? He's a towering man who can play basketball better than anyone around today. He's Kareem Abdul-Jabbar, who found himself in the Islamic faith, and discovered a whole new ball game in the Game of Life.

RICK BARRY

Some people paste labels all over their luggage to advertise the places they've visited. If Rick Barry ever decided to do that, he'd need a suitcase the size of Alaska.

Barry has been a basketball vagabond, bouncing from San Francisco to Oakland, to Washington, to Virginia, to New York, and back to the San Francisco-Oakland area. He has put on one super traveling show, shooting the eye out of the basket in whatever city or league he has played. Rick is the only man who led both the National and American Basketball Associations in scoring.

But a basketball player does not live by points alone. There are other factors to be judged—defense and playmaking, for example. Few men have been able to dominate more than one of these areas. Last season, having conquered scoring, Barry decided to work on the other areas. Suddenly, therefore, the Golden State shooting machine stopped making points. He started setting picks, making feeds to teammates, playing hard-nosed defense. It was as if he was saying, "Hey look, I can do other things besides score points."

His performance was convincing, but there was one small problem. The Warriors couldn't win without Barry's points. When some friends convinced Rick of that, he threw off the wraps and poured points like the Barry whom Franklin Mieuli had come to know and love.

Mieuli is the owner of the Warriors. He has only a few passions in life. One is riding motorcycles around northern California. Another is Richard Francis Barry III. When Barry left the Warriors in 1967, Mieuli took strong action. He pledged not to shave until Barry returned to the club. He hung Rick's empty No. 24 jersey in his office, pledging to fill it again with Barry.

"I loved him like a son," explained Mieuli. But like sons sometimes do, Rick strayed. Of course he had some help. The new ABA installed Bruce Hale, Barry's father-in-law and ex-coach at the University of Miami, as boss of its new Oakland franchise, and Rick jumped to the new circuit.

He sat out one season because of legal roadblocks—a terrible thing to befall a shooter of Barry's caliber. Then, the financially strapped Oakland Oaks moved

3,000 miles east to Washington, D.C. That lasted only one year before the franchise was moved again, this time to Virginia.

By then, Barry was getting used to traveling, but the trip to Virginia riled Rick. When he first left Mieuli's cozy club in the Bay Area, Barry never anticipated becoming part of a regional franchise that played home games all over the state. So Rick took a firm stand, publicly criticizing everything in the state of Virginia from the schools to the fans to the team. He created an untenable situation for the club's owners, who were virtually forced to peddle him to the New York Nets.

It was with the Nets that Barry seemed to find a home. He became the leader of the team and was appreciated by the sophisticated New York fans, who take their basketball seriously, whether watching the Knicks in Madison Square Garden, the Nets in the Nassau Coliseum or a pickup game in a schoolyard.

In New York, Barry turned the fans on and the fans did the same for him. The basketball gypsy appeared to have found a permanent home at last when old friend Franklin Mieuli surfaced again with a full-grown beard on his face and a court order in his hand.

In the midst of his ABA travels, Barry had become disillusioned and signed a contract with Mieuli, agreeing to return to the Warriors when his ABA obligations were completed. The date was in the far-off future when Barry signed the document but Mieuli kept ripping calendar pages, biding his time. Finally Franklin came around to collect his prize.

Roy Boe, owner of the Nets, tried to buy Rick's freedom. Barry tried to buy his own freedom. But Mieuli was having none of that. After a summer-long tussle, the Nets and Barry gave up and Rick returned to the Warriors for the 1972-73 season. The surrender wasn't exactly swift. Barry missed almost all of training camp before finally reporting to the Warriors. It showed in his play and he finished with a 22.3 average, lowest in his pro career.

The season wasn't a total washout. He started for the West in the All Star game, had a regular season string of 39 straight free throws and had a .902 foul shooting percentage for the campaign, fifth man in NBA history to top the .900 mark. He had a 50-point game, and in another game, he scored 24 points in one quarter.

But Barry felt he could and would do better in 1973-74. "Just being here when the team went to training camp is one thing," said Barry. "Last year, the first five or six weeks of the regular season was training camp for me."

Rick also felt that he had a better idea what his job with the Warriors should be. "When I showed up last year, I wasn't sure what role I should fill," he said. "I think the team wasn't sure which role I was going to fill. Consequently, it took awhile for us to adjust to each other."

It was in training camp that Barry decided to show good, all-around basketball player—a forward who does all the things he's supposed to do. I don't want to be remembered as a bad defensive player."

At the start of the season, Barry did not score a lot of points. "I guess people think I wasn't playing well the first half of the season because I didn't score a lot of points. It had to do with my style of play. I tried to do what I thought would help the team the most. I passed the ball, maybe more than I should have. I 30 field goals. Both were individual player highs for the his other basketball abilities. "We have so many fine shooters and scorers that I can help out on other things," he said. "I hope people remember me as a passed up shots that maybe I should have taken."

It was a complete about-face for Barry, who had

never been shy about shooting before. "I accepted it because I thought it would help," he explained. But it didn't help. Instead of flourishing, the Warriors floundered. Eventually, Barry and Coach Al Attles agreed that if the Warriors were to win, Barry would have to score points.

"One of the rules of basketball," said Barry, "is, if you can get a shot, take it, provided you don't have a teammate with a better shot. I can honestly say I never intentionally failed to throw a ball to a teammate who had a better shot than I did."

When Barry began shooting again, the ball kept going through the basket. Late in the season, he poured in 64 points in a game against Portland, connecting on NBA season.

He finished the season with a 25.1 average, sixth best in the league, and was the No. 2 foul shooter with an .899 percentage. His name also showed up among the leaders in a couple of other statistical categories. He averaged better than six assists per game and had 169 steals. That confirms his contention that he is not only a scorer but a well-rounded player as well.

"I think I have matured," he said. "I think I'm a better player today than I've ever been before."

Coach Attles agrees. "Barry is playing better than ever," he said. "The trouble is he does it so effortlessly that some fans don't appreciate how hard he is working."

One person appreciates every graceful maneuver: owner Mieuli, who believes that, like Dolly Levi, Rick Barry is back home where he belongs.

DAVE COWENS

Dave Cowens plays center like a perpetual motion machine with its switch stuck in the "on" position. He doesn't trot from one end of the court to the other in the tradition of the dominating big man who knows the offense will wait for him. Instead, Cowens dashes downcourt, dives for loose balls and plays with a zest that displays no concern for life or limb—least of all his own.

If the Boston Celtics' running game could be portrayed as a man's body, Cowens would be its heart, pumping away, keeping all the parts supplied with their needs. The suggestion brings a smile to the big redhead.

"You should have seen me in high school," he said. "I was a real wild man then. I guess I always played hard. It always came natural. The way I see it, you play hard and try to have a good time. Every team I played on was coached with that philosophy in mind."

The Celtics found Cowens hidden away in Florida State University, well camouflaged because his school was ineligible for NCAA tournaments, the penalty for some shabby recruiting violations. "He scared me to death the one time I scouted him," said Boston major domo Red Auerbach. "He was so good ... I kept hoping he'd make a mistake. There were half a dozen guys from other NBA clubs in the building, and I figured if they saw the same potential in Cowens I did, I was dead."

The year was 1969-70 and Boston, playing without

the newly retired Bill Russell, struggled to its worst record in 20 years. That dubious achievement did have one saving quality though. It insured the Celts a high draft choice—high enough to collar Cowens.

The choice was an obvious one. The absence of Russell had left Boston with an awesome gap at center. The solution, obviously, was to draft a center and Cowens was, of course, a center. There was, however, one problem. Cowens stands 6-foot-9, and while that's fine for a center in college, it's a bit on the short side for a man in the middle in the NBA, where seven-footers abound.

"My original estimate was he'd probably be a forward and part-time center," recalled Auerbach. "What changed my mind was his attitude. We could see right away in his first training camp that nobody was going to tell this kid he couldn't do something if he wanted to."

Auerbach decided to consult an expert. So he called in Boston's obvious consultant on centers—Russell, who was, significantly, also only 6-9.

"I called Russell for a quick opinion," said Auerbach. "Russ told us to forget Dave's height and let him play where he wanted. 'You won't be sorry,' he said. 'No one's going to intimidate that kid.' "

Intimidation. That's the word you think of when you think about the giants who play center in the NBA. It is Kareem Abdul-Jabbar batting the ball back down in the face of the shooter or Nate Thurmond soaring high to dunk a shot. Cowens recognized the task he was up against when he arrived in the NBA pivot to face those resident giants.

"I feel less talented than a lot of the guys I play against," said Dave, "and I know that most of them are a lot taller. But I can run the 100-yard dash with anyone in the league. To be effective, I've got to use my speed all the time. I've got to force the bigger guys out of their usual patterns and into mine by making them afraid that I'll run away from them and score easy baskets. They seem very conscious of my speed now. They're chasing me harder all the time. I started running because I didn't want them to embarrass me, and now they're running so I won't embarrass them."

K.C. Jones, coach of the Washington Bullets, remembers how that other 6-9, Boston center, operated. "Russell would intimidate you by blocking shots," said Jones, a longtime Celtic teammate of Russell's. "Dave Cowens intimidates you with his hustle. He blocks shots, dives after loose balls and never stops running. You don't find people his size doing that."

In essence, what Cowens does is play center like a guard. Other centers, and even some guards, have noticed.

"He does everything," said Nate Thurmond of the Golden State Warriors, who is 6-11. "He's made up for his height deficiency by the way he plays. I admire him because of it. Besides, I never faced a center who hustled the way he does. He's the toughest man I've ever played against."

Guard Norm Van Lier of Chicago often runs into Cowens outside, where you'd seldom expect to find the other team's center. "He adds a different dimension to Boston's game," said Van Lier. "He has great defensive range on a horizontal rather than on a vertical plane. He'll meet me at the top of the key, spread those long arms and make it almost impossible to pass off without him getting a finger on the ball."

Cowens is very straightforward about his approach to playing center in the NBA.

"My style is basically pretty simple," he said. "Since the guys I play against are usually bigger and stronger than me, in order for me to contribute, I play a fundamental game. That means I go for loose balls and hustle. If I played a lackadaisical game, I would not be of any use."

Cowens need not worry about that. In his first season he was co-Rookie of the Year with Portland's Geoff Petrie, and was the league's Most Valuable Player just two years later. He has scored and rebounded every bit as well as Russell suspected he would and has given the Celtics an extra edge with the intangibles he brings along for each game. Call that No. 1 intangible aggressiveness.

"It's the only way I can play because if I don't fight for the positions I want, the big guys will eat me up," said Cowens. "It's absolutely necessary that I box out on every play, even if it means I might not have a chance for the rebound. By keeping my own man off the boards, I know I've increased the odds that one of our other guys, like Paul Silas or Don Chaney, will get the ball."

That's called teamwork, and it's one of the things Cowens likes most about his life on the court.

"Playing basketball is one of the things I do best," he said. "I like the competition and I like the responsibility of being part of a team. There are immediate rewards for me in basketball. Scoring a basket for me is success. Missing is failure. I work to get open, throw a fake and score. The important thing for me is that in basketball I'm taking positive action. I have a goal and everything I do is pointed to that goal."

As a team, the Celtics achieved their goal last season when they won the NBA championship for the first time since the Russell era. John Havlicek was voted the MVP of the playoffs but Cowens, who dueled Abdul-Jabbar on almost equal terms in the final series, wasn't far behind.

After the playoffs, Cowens returned to his simple

Kentucky's Artis Gilmore led all ABA rebounders with better than 18 per game.

Bob Lanier (16) was named Most Valuable Player in the NBA All Star game.

Elvin Hayes discovered religion before last season and then led all NBA rebounders with 18.1 per game.

John Havlicek (17) was Boston's leading scorer with 22.6 points last season, 10th best in the league.

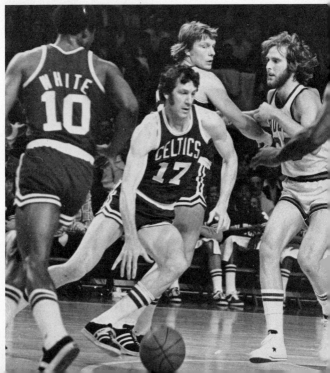

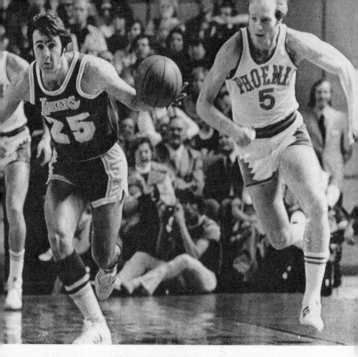

Gail Goodrich (25) of Los Angeles was the NBA's fifth highest scorer with a 25.3 point per game average.

Dan Issel's defense has often been criticized, but his scoring (25.5 last year) has never been questioned.

Powerful George Mc-
Ginnis averaged 26
points per game for
Indiana last year.

Buffalo's Bob McAdoo
(11) was Rookie of
the Year two seasons
ago and won the NBA
scoring crown last
year.

Walt Frazier drives for two against Boston. Clyde led the New York Knicks with 20.5 points per game.

Seattle's Spencer Haywood drives past Kareem Abdul-Jabbar. High scorer Haywood also had 13.4 rebounds per game!

Buffalo's Ernie Di-Gregorio (15) was chosen the NBA's rookie of the year and led the league in assists and foul shooting.

Rick Barry led Golden State in scoring last season, averaging better than 25 points per game.

Dr. J. operates. Julius Erving was the American Basketball Association's Most Valuable Player last year.

Dave Cowens (18) was the NBA's second best rebounder last season, even though he's "only" 6-foot-9.

It's up, up and away for Milwaukee's Kareem Abdul-Jabbar, the NBA's Most Valuable Player last season.

off-court existence. He does not favor the flamboyance so prevalent in the living style of many of today's pro basketball stars.

"Despite all my activity on the court, off the court I'm actually a passive person," he said. "In a way, I'm actually a very insecure person. I'm fortunate. How many other jobs can you work for eight months and have four months vacation? My hours are good and so is the pay. All I have to do is play a game."

It sounds simple, but very few play that game like this perpetual motion big red machine with the stuck starter switch.

ERNIE DiGREGORIO

If you take $2,300,000 and spread it over five years, simple arithmetic will give you $460,000 for each of those years. That is just about what the Buffalo Braves are paying Ernie DiGregorio, and the little guy from Providence College paid them handsome dividends the first year of their investment.

Ernie D. led the National Basketball Association in assists and free throws in 1973-74, and it's no coincidence that the Braves made the playoffs for the first time ever in their flashy backcourt man's first season. He was the Rookie of the Year and the acknowledged floor leader of the young and talented Buffalo club.

It wasn't the easiest transition from scorer at Providence to playmaker at Buffalo. It took work, but work never bothered Ernie, who spent endless hours in playgrounds and gymnasiums, dribbling and shooting—refining his court talents.

"It's true that I've had to temper my game a little in the pros," said DiGregorio. "I can't think only of offense. When I was in high school and college, the offense was designed for me to look for the basket and shoot, and the other players were supposed to look for me."

The idea at Buffalo was for Ernie D. to run the offense and look for the other guys—shooters like Jim McMillian, Bob McAdoo and the rest of the Braves' cast. "There's a lot of pressure on him and there hasn't been a kid to come into this league and be able to run the show consistently since Oscar Robertson," said Eddie Donovan, general manager of the Braves.

Donovan saw something in Ernie that made him believe this young man had the tools to do the job the Braves needed. "The only way Ernie is going to learn is to play. OK, so he'll make his share of mistakes and we expect that . . . rookies are inconsistent. Yes, even the best, and we consider him the best. But Ernie is going to get better and that means we'll get better."

Early in his rookie season, DiGregorio got burned by Jerry West, who took advantage of Ernie's defensive lapses to score 36 points against the young man. That was when the whispers started. The D in Ernie D. should be no-D for no defense, they said. And Ernie heard every one of those slurs.

"Sure, I've heard the talk about my defense," he nodded. "Anytime anybody says something about it, it offends me. I'm still finding my way around the league . . . there's a lot to learn. I'll be a lot better player later on, believe me."

Then DiGregorio paused. "You know," he said, "I'll bet West scored 36 and more on guys better than me." But those other players weren't making 460 big ones every year, and DiGregorio recognized that factor. "I just think that those who look at people who are making a lot of money and are well publicized have to find something wrong. I think it was just something they picked out to say about my defense. If you looked at every player in the NBA, and looked for a single weakness, you could find anything if you looked close enough," he said.

If you looked close enough at Ernie D., you'd think that D stood for dedication, because that is what this six-foot shrimp brought with him to the giant-sized world of the NBA.

When he was 11 years old, DiGregorio decided that basketball was his game.

"If you're going to be any good," he once philosophized about his game, "You have to work harder than the other person. And if that means playing basketball six or seven or eight hours a day with never more than one day off in a row for 10, 11, 12 years, that's the price you pay."

Ernie paid. "People used to think I was crazy," he recalled. "They even said I wasn't going to look like a man when I grew up, but like a basketball. I dribbled a basketball everywhere. Even when I went to my girlfriend's house to pick her up, I'd have a basketball with me."

It didn't matter to Ernie whether there were enough kids around for a game or scrimmage, or whether he was by himself, alone with that round ball. "I practiced mostly alone, six and seven hours a day. I'd be up at six in the morning sometimes to get in a few hours before school. Basketball isn't all luck. It's work, long, hard hours of work. But like everything else, if you want to be the best, there's a price. Right?"

Ernie knew the price and paid it. "If you work at it, you've got to be better. I know how much work I put in, so the guy against me can't be better. No way he can be better," he insisted.

That solid conviction that he is the best was jolted after his junior year at Providence. The powers that be didn't even invite the snub-nosed backcourtman to try out for the Olympic team. DiGregorio's pride was hurt, and he made up his mind to show the selectors they had made a mistake. "I wanted to go out and prove that I was one of the best guards in the country," he said. So, in his senior season, he averaged 18 points per game, was named to the All America team, won the Joe Lapchick Award as the outstanding collegiate senior, and led Providence to the semifinals of the NCAA Tournament. Then he capped the season with a dazzling show for the United States team, leading America's collegians to four victories in six games against the touring Russian team—the same Russians who had beaten the Americans, without DiGregorio, in the Olympics.

"It was all very satisfying," said DiGregorio. It got even more satisfying when Buffalo in the NBA and Kentucky in the ABA drafted him and started waving handfuls of money in front of him. "I really wanted to play in the NBA," said DiGregorio, "but when people go crazy with money like Kentucky did, you've got to listen." Eventually, though, Ernie put his autograph on a Buffalo contract.

Early in the pre-season, Coach Jack Ramsay ran an intrasquad game, sending his rookies, led by DiGregorio, against Buffalo's veterans. Ernie D. scored 34 points, pacing the newcomers' victory.

"That's when Ernie established himself as our floor leader," said Ramsay. "I wanted him to earn that distinction on the court, and he showed he deserved it."

On the court, Ernie spent the first month of the season getting acclimated to the NBA and his new role.

"In college, I was allowed to freelance. People set picks for me," he said. "Here, we use set plays except for the fast break. I don't have the freedom I had in college."

The adjustment took time but DiGregorio made it fairly smoothly. Soon he was leading the league in assists and free throw shooting, and not at all surprised by his success.

"The things I can do, I have confidence in," he said. "In college, I used to check the NBA statistics in the newspapers every week and see where the assists leader was averaging eight or nine a game. I was doing that at Providence and I thought, if the rebounders in the NBA got the ball to me on the fast break, I could average that too. I know I can pass."

Result: 663 assists, 8.2 per game, best in the league.

"Free throws are just concentration, practice and rhythm," he added. "You get into the groove."

Result: 174 of 193 free throw shots made, .902 percentage, best in the league.

Does hard work pay off? Ernie DiGregorio is walking . . . make that dribbling . . . proof that it does.

JULIUS ERVING

It is a measure of how much Julius Erving has accomplished in his three years of professional basketball that he is rarely called by his proper name—first or last. Seldom do you hear him referred to as "Julius" or "Erving." Instead, it's "The Doctor" or "Doc" or "Dr. J." The nickname is all the identity he needs. Once you've seen him operate, you don't forget it easily.

The good doctor has won the ABA scoring championship in each of the last two seasons and was the league's most valuable player both in the 1973-74 regular season and playoffs as he led the New York Nets first to the best record in the ABA and then to the playoff championship as well.

Other players have averaged as much as and more than the 27.4 points per game that earned Dr. J. his second scoring title last year. But few have done it as spectacularly. The Doctor is the ultimate basketball entertainer. He does things on a court that others wouldn't even try. He has a flair, a dynamic style that makes him stand out from other pro basketball players. Kareem Abdul-Jabbar stands out because he's more than seven feet tall. Erving is an almost mortal-sized (for basketball) 6-6, but his performance on the court makes him stand out every bit as much as Jabbar.

Besides his scoring title last season, Dr. J. was among the league's top 10 leaders in five other departments—rebounds, assists, blocked shots, steals and field goal percentage. He made the $4,000,000 deal Nets' owner Roy Boe negotiated to bring Erving to New York seem like a bargain basement price.

It would have been much cheaper for Boe if the Nets had said yes to Erving the first time they had the chance. It was in 1971, and Erving had finished his junior season at the University of Massachusetts and decided it was time to turn pro. What better place than on Long Island with the Nets? After all, Erving had grown up in Roosevelt, only a few miles from Uniondale and the Nassau Coliseum, where the Nets play their home games. It seemed a natural. At least, Dr. J. thought so.

He called Lou Carnesecca, the peppery little ex-collegiate coach who was general manager-coach of the Nets at that time. Now Carnesecca was as interested as the next guy in building a top team, and he knew how much Dr. J. could mean to that effort. But Lou also has an unalterable commitment to education, probably as a result of his long experience as a high school and collegiate educator. So, as hard as it was to do from a basketball standpoint, Carnesecca said no to Erving, strictly from an educational standpoint. It was his unbreakable rule. He simply wouldn't sign an underclassman and nothing could change that position—not even a player with the obvious talent of a Julius Erving.

Rejected by the Nets, Dr. J. went shopping elsewhere. It didn't take him long to find another team that wasn't quite as interested in whether he had his degree. Where Carnesecca had said no, the Virginia Squires gave Erving a resounding yes. The package was four years for $500,000. The payments were to be spread over seven years and The Doctor thought he was set.

"I signed because I wanted to help myself and my family," he revealed. "I looked at myself and said, 'Man, I've got a half million. I can do anything I want.' But it wasn't so."

There were all kinds of problems for Dr. J. Deferred payments reduced the actual amount of money he saw. He signed in March but payments weren't to begin until November, leaving the supposedly wealthy young basketball player with eight months of empty pockets. He was uneasy, to say the least. "I didn't have money to live on," he said. So he borrowed from the Squires and they started taking the loans back during Erving's first few months with the club. "More money was going out than coming in," he said.

Erving's financial problems wound up in the lap of business manager Irwin Weiner and the decision was made to attempt to renegotiate his contract. There was no shortage of teams interested in that idea, even if Virginia wasn't one of them. The best offer came from the Atlanta Hawks of the NBA—something like $2,000,000 for five years plus a $250,000 bonus and a few other fringe benefits.

The next step was a legal one—an attempt to sue the Squires to win his freedom. Erving claimed that one of the agents representing him in his original signing with the Squires was really a double agent, paid by Virginia to direct talent to the team. That was a violation of the rules. Then the Milwaukee Bucks added further confusion to the situation by drafting Erving's NBA rights—a little matter Atlanta had failed to do.

That created one dandy three-way tug of war, but the hassle hardly disturbed Erving's carefully nurtured Afro. Dr. J. left the matter in the hands of a court-appointed referee. Archibald Cox, who was to be heard from later as special prosecutor in the Watergate case, was the man who would decide Dr. J.'s future. Meanwhile, Erving went about his business, leading all ABA scorers and emerging as the league's most glamorous player. He was cool about the contract problem.

"If my contract with Virginia is not valid," he said, "I'll go to Atlanta. If it is valid, the Atlanta contract will take effect after two years. As far as Milwaukee goes, I don't know what's going to happen."

Whatever Cox decided, it seemed obvious that, sooner or later, Erving would be leaving the ABA and going across to the other league to do his thing. Enter Roy Boe, one of the ABA's most dynamic owners. Losing Erving to the NBA didn't sit well with Boe, and so he went to work on the problem. It wasn't easy. Worthwhile projects seldom are.

"At the end, we had seven lawyers working on it," said Boe. "It was like closing for a house."

"It was more like closing for a bank," countered Weiner.

The Nets packaged something like a half-million dollars to pacify Atlanta and gave the Squires a couple of ballplayers and another three quarters of a million. Then the Nets signed Doctor J. to an eight-year contract worth another $2,800,000.

The deal delighted Erving because Long Island is his home and, after all, that's where he wanted to play in the first place. Anyone will tell you that a contented basketball player performs better than an unhappy one, and Dr. J. was certainly contented.

His season reflected that contentment. He was everything the Nets could hope for and then some. Even he recognized it. "By far this has been my best all-around season and I feel as though it helps bring me a step closer to realizing some of the goals I set for myself when I came into this profession. I want to be acknowledged as one of the best players who has played the game," he said.

Certainly, he has already attained that distinction, not only from fans and press, but from his peers—the other players.

"Dr. J. is the only man with a PhD in basketball," a former teammate has said. "He's a surgeon. Just give him the ball, and watch him operate."

WALT FRAZIER

He has hands that resemble a snake's tongue, moving swiftly and suddenly to strike out at a foe. He has fingers that lick out at the ball like a flame, feeding on fuel. He is Walt "Clyde" Frazier, the heart and soul of the New York Knicks.

Clyde is only a nickname, hung on him by team-mates several years ago because his flamboyant taste in clothing seemed reminiscent of Clyde Barrow, the bank robber of the Thirties. But he wears the name proudly, as a badge identifying him as "cool." And if there is one thing that Frazier is, it is cool.

Just what is this thing called cool that is so much identified with Frazier? Let Clyde explain. "Cool is reactions," he said, "reflexes and attitude. You got to feel out the situation. You can't be out of control."

Perish the thought that Clyde would ever be out of control. He tried it once during the 1974 playoffs when he produced distinctly un-Frazier-like performances in the early games of the Knicks' first-round series against the Capital Bullets. He was rewarded for his uncharacteristic efforts with a chorus of boos from basketball sophisticates who attend the games in New York's Madison Square Garden. They let Clyde have it good. Clearly, Clyde's reputation and past performance chart were working against him. He had established a level of excellence and the fans would accept nothing less than that from him.

"Getting booed hurt my pride," Frazier admitted. "You know, it took me seven years to get to the top. I consider myself the number one guard in basketball. One or two bad playoff games can't destroy what seven years has built."

What bothered Frazier most was that other players have had bad games, even bad series, without being blistered the way the New York fans had blistered him. "No matter what I do," noted Frazier, "I keep having to prove myself."

So, Clyde proved himself. He destroyed the Bullets with 38 points in the fifth game of the series and afterwards he talked about his feelings and his special chemistry with the fans.

"Two weeks before the end of the season, I decided to stop eating potatoes, bread and desserts," he said. "I lost about five pounds. That's when my shot started to go off. I was lighter and didn't feel in control of my body."

When that happened, Clyde went back to the table, "eating like I normally do—like a pig." Still, his game was slightly out of balance and it showed. Everybody noticed because, after all, Clyde is the last guy you'd expect to be having problems on the court.

"Guys who never speak to me . . . guys like the doorman came up to me and said, 'I heard you almost blew the game.'" That was after Frazier's ill-advised layup attempt against Elvin Hayes in the final seconds of game four. "That's all I need to hear before I go to sleep."

Frazier bounced back, overwhelming the Bullets in game five. "Once I hit a couple of shots and heard the cheers, I got my confidence, my rhythm back. Everything was quick and up . . . no thinking about it."

Then Clyde smiled. "A game like this just sets me up for more criticism," he said. "I can't win. If I do, I'm supposed to. If I don't, I'm to blame. But I don't hold any grudge against the fans. I'm too nice a guy for that."

He's also too talented to worry about an off game here or there. "He has his pride," said Coach Red Holzman. "He likes to think he's one of the best players in the league. And he is."

"Clyde owns the ball," said Willis Reed, captain of the Knicks. "He just loans it to the rest of us once in a while."

That's exactly the way it seems to develop, game after game. Frazier brings the ball down court, rarely racing but usually drifting instead. He is in control, totally in charge. "Coming down with the ball," he said,

"I usually don't know what's going to happen when I cross the half-court line. I don't make up my mind that I'm going to shoot or that I'm going to pass. I just go. Whatever happens, happens. We're working together to get a man open for a jump shot or spring a guy loose for a drive. It's like making up something—making a poem or something. You're in control . . . and it's going to be exciting. That's one of the joys of basketball—improvising. The amazing thing about making a move is that I might never have made it before and I might never make it again. It's just happening, then and there."

It's been happening for Clyde ever since 1966, when he led Southern Illinois to the championship of the National Invitation Tournament at Madison Square Garden. Frazier was all over the place, scoring 88 points, grabbing 52 rebounds and picking up 19 assists in four games. He was the tournament's most valuable player, an honor he called "my biggest thrill," and he opened the eyes of the Knicks' executives.

"I was surprised when they drafted me," said Frazier. "They had a lot of other guards at the time." But none of them could run a team the way Clyde could, and he quickly won a job with the Knicks. His arrival in New York parallels the beginnings of the Knickerbockers as an NBA powerhouse.

As he and the Knicks moved up in the world, Frazier steadily improved his life style. He moved into a penthouse apartment on Manhattan's fashionable East Side and furnished the pad with, among other things, a mink-covered round bed. The closets were stocked with 25 suits, a modest total for a man of his sartorial splendor. "I never keep more than that," he said. "I get disenchanted with them if I have too many." There were six fur coats, 60 shirts and about 100 pairs of shoes.

He owns a $20,000 Rolls-Royce and employs a chauffeur to drive him around the city. But he uses the subway to ride to work. "I don't like the traffic hassle," he said.

Clyde is a loner off the court. He shuns crowds, preferring to stay out of the spotlight when he is not working. "I don't like to travel with an entourage," he said. "I've always been my own man."

There is a good reason why Frazier enjoys being alone. It is a privilege he didn't enjoy as a youngster growing up in Atlanta. He was the oldest of nine children and has seven sisters and one brother. In high school, Frazier played basketball and football and it was there that he discovered how fickle fans can be. "Something happened that gave me a perspective on all this," he said. "On what you can expect from people when you're an athlete and don't produce."

What happened was that Frazier inherited his football team's quarterbacking job when the regular passer was injured. He was neither ready for the challenge nor capable of handling it. "We didn't win before me and we didn't win with me that season," he said.

The next season, Frazier threw 16 touchdown passes, leading the school to the city championship. He was now the hero of the school, and that sudden turnabout taught Clyde that you're only as good as your last game. What went before that really doesn't matter.

It is a lesson he has not forgotten.

Since coming into the NBA, Frazier has been considered the epitome of cool. He even authored a book on the subject called *Rockin' Steady, a Guide to Basketball and Cool.* No one knows more about the subject than the man they call Clyde. He is the coolest.

ARTIS GILMORE

Artis Gilmore lives under the basket, a perfectly natural place for any man who is 7-feet, 2-inches tall. He also lives in a fishbowl, also perfectly natural for a man 7-foot-2. He prefers the former but accepts the latter.

The goateed Kentucky Colonels' giant once stepped out of a midtown New York restaurant when a sharp-eyed passerby picked him right out of the crowd.

"Are you an athlete?" the friendly citizen asked.

"Yes," replied Gilmore. "I'm a hockey player—a goalie."

Another time, Artis was strolling through an airport, toting a teammate's tennis racquet. He was noticed, naturally, and overheard two fans speculating on just who that big guy with the racquet might be.

"I'm Arthur Ashe," he offered, never breaking stride.

Gilmore may be amusing off the court, but he's no joke to the other team when he steps on the court. He has become one of professional basketball's most dominating centers, a giant of a man whose mere presence has an intimidating effect on ambitious opponents,

Big Artis has been in the ABA for three seasons and he has led the league in rebounding in each of those seasons. Drafted out of Jacksonville University, Gilmore represented something of a gamble on the part of the Colonels, who invested about $2,000,000 in him. Utah Coach Joe Mullaney was Kentucky's bench boss when the Colonels selected Gilmore, and he remembers the soul-searching the club went through before picking the big guy.

"I remember ... hearing that the scouts had Artis rated pretty low," said Mullaney. "They had him behind Elmore Smith of Kentucky State and (Jim) McDaniels (of Western Kentucky) and one other guy, I think. There were mixed feelings about Artis in college —a general opinion that he was good, but maybe not unusually good.

"I saw him twice on TV myself so I knew that he was a fine defensive player, but I had my doubts about his offensive abilities."

Kentucky's general manager then was Mike Storen, now commissioner of the ABA. He was under great pressure to choose McDaniels, not only because of the doubts about Gilmore, but because McDaniels represented a hometown hero for Kentucky fans. Storen, however, stayed with Gilmore. McDaniels, drafted by Carolina, later jumped to Seattle of the NBA and ultimately was cut by the SuperSonics. Gilmore, meanwhile, flourished with the Colonels and helped the team to the earliest division clinching in ABA history. He led the league in three statistical departments—blocked shots (422), rebounding (17.8 per game), and two-point field goal percentage (59.8). He won both Rookie of the Year and Most Valuable Player honors!

"No one dreamed Artis would do as much as he did," confessed Mullaney. Wrong. Gilmore nurtured such grandiose dreams.

"I want to be the greatest player who ever played the game," said Gilmore. "I don't know if I'll ever reach that objective, but I'm not being fair to myself or my team if I don't point in that direction. I feel a man should have only one goal. And that is to be the very best."

There are those around the ABA who believe that Gilmore has achieved that goal and that he is every bit as good as the best centers in the NBA—Jabbar, Thurmond, Unseld, Cowens and McAdoo.

Bill Sharman, coach of the Los Angeles Lakers, doesn't have to worry about Gilmore because his team operates in the other league. But that doesn't limit his respect and admiration for Kentucky's Big A.

"Artis Gilmore will be to the Colonels what Bill Russell was to the Boston Celtics," said Sharman, himself a longtime teammate of Russell's with the Celts. "An intimidating defensive player who can set up their fast breaks and allow a great player like Dan Issel to concentrate more on offense."

Issel was the Colonels' center until Artis arrived on the scene. Dan was delighted with Gilmore's rapid development. "He makes life a lot easier for me now," said Issel. "I don't have to worry about rebounding as much and he's made us all look a lot tougher on defense. I never saw Mr. Russell in person, but I don't see how anyone can get as high as Gilmore."

When Gilmore came into the league, he opened a lot of eyes in a hurry. "He is a presence," said Coach Mullaney. "You're always aware the big guy is there," said Lou Carnesecca, then coach of the New York Nets. "You look for him out of the corner of your eye. You know he's there . . . somewhere." Tom Nissalke, coach of the San Antonio Spurs, said the price Kentucky paid for Gilmore's autograph on a contract was cheap. "Two million . . . it was the biggest steal in history," he said. "For two million, Kentucky bought a basketball team for 10 years."

Gilmore brought plenty of confidence with him when he moved into the ABA. "Every time I walk out on the court," he said, "I plan to win. When I go on the court, I feel I should get every jump ball. At a certain point, I have a feeling I have to get the ball. When you are continuously getting rebounds, you feel it's automatic that you'll get the next one."

Gilmore came into the league anxious to leave his mark. "I like honors," he said. "I'd like to set some records, and then more and more records. I like records."

In his first year alone, Gilmore shattered nine Kentucky club standards. Last season, he set an ABA record when he grabbed 40 rebounds in a single game at New York. Afterwards, Coach Babe McCarthy suggested that Artis hadn't reached his peak yet. "Most players keep improving until they're 27," said McCarthy. Gilmore is only 25.

It was only a decade ago that the big, gangly teenager was growing up in a ghetto section of Chipley, Florida, one of nine children living in a cold-water flat that didn't even have electricity. His family moved to Alabama and he averaged 38 points a game in Carver High School at Dolthan. He was 6-8 then, and didn't really think that much of himself as a player. "I had no talent, considering the other ballplayers on my team," he said.

After high school, Gilmore attended Gardner Webb Junior College before going to Jacksonville. It was with the college team that he began attracting national attention.

Gilmore still seemed a little rough around the edges when he first came to the Colonels, and even after three star-studded seasons, the club believes he can be even better than he is, and so does he.

"I guess I'm never really satisfied with my performance," said Gilmore. "I don't believe in personal goals, isolated goals which relate to a game or a season. If you do that, and you accomplish those goals, then I feel you lose your incentive. If you reach the top of the mountain, then there's no place else to go, so you set your sights on the highest mountain and hope someday you'll reach it."

Bud Olsen, assistant coach of the Colonels last season, thinks Artis is getting there. "I said before last season started that Artis is at about 60% of his full potential," said Olsen. "Now I would say a conservative estimate would be closer to 75%. He's going to get better because of his attitude. He's very coachable and anxious—hungry, really—to be the best that's ever played the game."

GAIL GOODRICH

Gail Goodrich is a Lilliputian living in the redwood forest known as the National Basketball Association. He stands 6-foot-1 in a league where the average backcourt man towers 6-4 or 6-5. But that's still much better than the situation he faced coming out of high school, where he was a mere 5-7.

Goodrich enrolled in UCLA and by the time he had graduated, the Bruins were well on the way to a collegiate basketball dynasty. Meanwhile, the shrimp guard from the San Fernando Valley had stretched himself half a dozen inches. It was enough for the professional Los Angeles Lakers to gamble on him in the draft of college players.

Now that seemed to be the perfect pro beginning for Goodrich. He had been a Los Angeles high school star and he had starred there in college. With the Lakers, he would have a chance to complete the local triangle.

And really, that's all he wanted—a chance. But when you're a six-footer in the NBA, it's easy to get lost. And for three years, Goodrich was lost, stuck on the end of the bench. It made for a most unhappy professional baptism for him.

Goodrich has always been a stand-up guy and so he stood up and told the Lakers either to play him or trade him. They chose the latter, placing Goodrich in an expansion draft pool. "I didn't care where I went," said Gail, "just so I left the Lakers."

The Phoenix Suns selected him and Goodrich's confidence in himself paid dividends immediately. Installed in the Suns' backcourt, he flourished, leading the club in assists, and scoring more than 20 points per game in the team's first two seasons. He also played in the mid-season All Star Game and that was the worst thing that could have happened to him as far as Phoenix was concerned.

It was then that Goodrich learned the going salary rate for All Star guards in the NBA. It turned out to be considerably higher than the numbers on his contract and Gail decided it was time to stand up again. "Either improve the numbers," he told management, "or trade me." Again, the club chose the latter and dealt him. And where do you think he wound up? Why Los Angeles, naturally. The Lakers surrendered seven-foot Mel Counts to get Goodrich back and the Suns were pleased with the deal because they gained a tall man and lost a short one. What's more, Counts wasn't demanding the fancy "All-Star" contract that Goodrich wanted.

Goodrich wasn't exactly thrilled with the transaction. He remembered those three seasons on the end of the Lakers' bench all too well. But things were different this time. The Lakers let him have the basketball and gave him a spot in the starting lineup. Los Angeles had learned its lesson. Goodrich wasn't a benchwarmer anymore.

Five years in the league had changed Gail's style of play, too. "I remember when he first came into the league," said John Barnhill, a long-time NBA player and now an assistant coach. "He'd drive on anybody —even Bill Russell."

Russell had this annoying habit of driving layups right back in the face of ambitious little guards like Goodrich. "Russell would block his shot," recalled Barnhill, "but he'd come back and try it again." Eventually, though, Gail got the message and learned to get his shot off faster and increase its arc to get it over the hands of the defender.

In his first year back, Goodrich led the Lakers in assists. In the next three years, he led the club in scoring.

"Gail has one of the best techniques—if not the best—of any of the smaller guards for going to the basket," said Laker Coach Bill Sharman, a pretty good backcourtman in his day with the Boston Celtics. "He can get the shot off and get it through the hoop." And, after all, that is what this game is all about, isn't it?

"Also," Sharman continued, "he's working harder and is more dedicated on defense. He has very quick hands, so he steals a lot of passes."

Last season represented an important transition for Goodrich, who averaged 25.3 points per game, fifth best in the league. For most of the year, he had to work without his regular backcourt mate, the great Jerry West, sidelined by injuries. Before the season, Goodrich realized that eventually West would be gone. He considered the consequences when an observer suggested that West's presence in the lineup made Goodrich more effective.

"That's probably true," he said. "But that's also true of anybody on our team. Jerry is a great playmaker and I think we complemented each other well. We blended together and didn't hurt each other's games. I would be a better basketball player with anyone who had his talents. I don't think my role has changed that much with Jerry gone. I play best without the ball, moving and cutting."

Goodrich reached a personal milestone last season when he went over the 10,000-point career plateau, a rather impressive accomplishment for a player his size. "It was quite a thrill," he said, after announcement of the achievement prompted a lengthy standing ovation from the fans in Jack Kent Cooke's LA Forum. "I know a lot of people had doubts I'd ever get this far."

There is a tendency among players who score as much as Goodrich does to overlook the other end of the court where they are supposed to play defense. Don't include Gail in that group.

"If you compare my defense to my offense, it's obviously not as good," noted Goodrich. "But I think my defense is better than people give me credit for. Sure, people say I don't play defense. But I don't see a lot of guys scoring 30 points on me. And the guys who do score are scoring on everybody else, too."

Offensively, the Lakers look to Goodrich to put the ball in the hoop. West has slowed down. There's no more Wilt Chamberlain, no more Jim McMillian. It means that Goodrich must produce the points if LA is to win.

"I like to believe I'm a better shooter now than earlier in my career," he said. "I'm getting better at getting my shots. There's a difference between a pure shooter and a scorer. For example, I don't consider John Havlicek a pure shooter but he gets open to score. I would like to believe that I'm a shooter and a scorer."

After his first year back with the Lakers, Goodrich decided to return to UCLA for a conditioning program directed by the school's track coach, Jim Bush. The program was ambitious and succeeded in building Goodrich's legs up for the grind of both training camp and the regular season. When Coach Sharman ran the Lakers, many of them were huffing and puffing. But Gail had done his homework and handled the work load easily.

"Give the credit to Gail," said Bush, eventually hired as a consultant by Cooke for both the Lakers and hockey's LA Kings. "I just gave him some direction. He did the rest."

The thing Goodrich seeks more than anything else on a basketball court is consistency. It is a strong point he shares with many professional athletes.

"Basketball is a game of peaks and valleys," he said. "So you can't get too emotional over one ball game. For every high, there's going to be a low. The object is to be consistent every night. But over an 82-game schedule, it's difficult to retain the necessary level of concentration for every game."

Difficult, but not impossible, and Goodrich's night-in, night-out performances for the Lakers prove that.

JOHN HAVLICEK

The champagne glistened on his dark hair and some of it rolled down into his eyes, irritating them for the moment. John Havlicek didn't mind. He was enjoying every moment of his seventh world championship celebration with the Boston Celtics. Except, he was enjoying this one even more than the others.

"During the early years of my career with Boston, we looked to Bill Russell for the leadership," said Havlicek. Hondo, now 34, is one of the last remnants of the Russell years in Boston and is the veteran that these young Celtics follow. "This is the new Celtics and it's our first title," Havlicek continued. "Now the guys all look to me with respect for that leadership. And that makes this the most satisfying title of all."

Havlicek managed only 16 points in the seventh and deciding game of Boston's NBA championship series against Milwaukee last May 12. But that couldn't diminish the brilliance he displayed in the first six games of the Bucks series and earlier against the New York Knickerbockers and Buffalo Braves. That performance added up to selection as the playoffs' Most Valuable Player—a choice that provoked very little argument.

Havlicek seems to feel a much more integral part of these new Celtics than he did on the Russell teams that dominated the league during the 1960s. "I was absorbed on the other teams," he said. "But on this team, I started with a rebirth. The team began from scratch. We used to have 10 individuals who could each do a job. We have a younger, less experienced team now, but we're starting to achieve style that the old Celtics had. We're trying to keep alive the image of the running Celtics."

Often the Celts will charge downcourt with Jo Jo White or Don Chaney carrying the ball, holding one hand in the air to signal a play and calling "Ohio." That's the name of a play designed for Havlicek, who learned his basketball at Ohio State on great Buckeye teams that included Jerry Lucas, Larry Siegfried and Mel Nowell among others.

"I learned about defense in college," said Havlicek.

"Coach Fred Taylor had five guys at Ohio State who averaged more than 30 points in high school, so he needed a defensive forward. That was me."

Havlicek went about his task energetically, and while he was practicing defense, he learned a little something about offense. "I became aware that movement is the most important thing on offense. If I keep moving, the defensive man is going to have to work harder. If you keep in constant movement, something is going to happen, even if you run without purpose. You run to create situations."

At Ohio State, Havlicek recognized and accepted his situation. "In college, I was the guy who grinds it out," he said. "I was the person who doesn't receive the publicity of the scorer. I didn't shoot much."

Still, Havlicek was a first-rate athlete—the type of player who doesn't escape the notice of the scouts. Boston noticed, and John was the Celtics' first draft choice in 1962. Then an interesting wrinkle was added. The Cleveland Browns picked him on the seventh round of the National Football League draft, even though he had never played collegiate football. The plan was to try him at wide receiver. It intrigued John.

"I thought I had the best hands in camp," said Havlicek, a trace of a smile crossing his face at the memory of those days in the Cleveland training camp. "Not too many disagreed with me. And I had to run the 40-yard dash twice, because the first time I ran a 4.6 and they didn't believe it."

The choice for the Browns came down to Havlicek or Gary Collins and, really, it wasn't a hard decision to make. Collins had a no-cut contract. Havlicek, of course, was cut.

"Sure I was crushed," he said. "I felt the Browns had made a mistake. I felt I could really play."

He was right. He could play—basketball—and

the Celtics discovered that quickly when John showed up for their training camp.

"I started as a defensive specialist," said Havlicek, replaying the role he had in college. More wasn't required from him, especially on a team that included the great Russell, the Jones boys, K.C. and Sam, Bob Cousy, Tom Sanders, Tom Heinsohn and Frank Ramsey. But as the Celtics evolved, so did Havlicek.

"As you go through your career, your role changes," said John. "I moved on to replace Sam Jones as the sixth man and then to become the guy who has to take the important shot."

Through all the role changes one factor remained constant. Call it the Havlicek Habit. "I just play basketball," he said, "and it doesn't matter who is playing me. I'm still going to run and try to move without the ball. I'm a simple-minded person. I don't like to complicate my life. I play as hard as I can for as long as I can."

It's a simple formula, and Havlicek has utilized it while climbing to stardom. Midway through the 1973-74 season, he soared past the 20,000-point mark, becoming only the eighth player in NBA history to achieve that career scoring plateau. He was one of the least likely candidates for that kind of achievement when he first came into the league. To score that many points, you've got to shoot the ball. Havlicek, carrying over his collegiate habits, showed a reluctance to shoot.

Finally, Coach Red Auerbach decided to have a talk with his rookie flash. "You can't let them insult you," Auerback told Havlicek. "Shoot! They sag off when you've got the ball because they know you won't shoot. Show them you can."

"Red only had to tell me once," said Havlicek. "I knew I could shoot," he said. Soon the rest of the league knew it too. Then, slowly but surely, Havlicek's role with the Celtics became more important. One by one as the older players left, John inherited their roles. Russell was the last one to leave, and when he departed, Havlicek emerged as the total leader of the club, not only emotionally, but statistically as well. When Russell retired, John even led the club in the big man's specialty—rebounding. At 6-foot-5, he could make the play like a guard, take the shot like a forward and grab the rebound like a center. He was a one-man wrecking crew.

When his teammate, Tom Heinsohn, took over as coach, he revealed why he admired Havlicek's talents. "Even when he makes a gamble," said Heinsohn, "it's a good gamble. Center [Dave] Cowens will make a gamble, and if he loses, the guy will score. If John makes a gamble, he knows someone is going to be around to cover up. He's already checked that before he's moved."

Havlicek has had considerable experience. A 48-minute per game man, he operates nonstop—at both ends of the court.

"I get tired," he said. "Everybody gets tired. But what good does it do to say you're tired? I'm not as strong or fast as I used to be. But I'm more mature. I play with more purpose. I know when to break and turn it on."

Still, Havlicek realizes that some day his playing career will end just as the basketball longevity of Russell, Cousy, K.C. Jones, Sam Jones and the others ultimately ended.

"I've gone from the young guy to the old man," he said. "In fact, now I'm a senior citizen. One of these days, they're going to have to find somebody else to do my job."

That won't be easy. Few people do that job with the

zest and accomplishment of a Havlicek. "John is worth 50 points a game to us," said Heinsohn.

That's right—50 points! It only seems like more.

ELVIN HAYES

It was the summer of 1973 and Elvin Hayes, the enigmatic star of the Capital Bullets, was relaxing in his off-season home in Houston. One day, Hayes' wife, Erna, a deeply religious woman, asked Elvin to accompany her to services at the Bible Way Church of Holiness.

Something told the Big E to go along with his wife that day, and he'll tell you now it was the most important experience he has ever had. It was the turning point in his life. It was the day he found religion and, at the same time, himself.

Rev. J. L. Parker was preaching to his congregation when Hayes showed up. He summoned Elvin to the front of the church and proceeded to dazzle Hayes as he had seldom been dazzled. "He told me personal things about myself that no one else knew but me. These were things about myself that had never been printed and things that he couldn't possibly have found out from man. Only God could have revealed these things to him. It scared me a little.

"He said, 'The Lord knows you; the Lord loves you.' He said He had a message for me, but didn't know how to get through to me."

The Reverend Parker recommended some literature for Hayes and the Big E became a regular each Sunday at the Bible Way Church, where he says he talked to Jesus.

"I prayed in a closet and I asked Him to save me, and He touched my life immediately. I asked Him to save me, to clean me up of all the sins I have committed. It was like somebody having a rope on you and pulling it around your neck and tugging. The Lord talked to me and told me all my sins. He told me how He has opened doors for me and without Him I would fail."

Hayes believed. With all of his being, he believed. He remembers all too well what life was like for him before his religious awakening.

"I didn't find Jesus earlier because I wasn't ready," said Hayes. "God will let a man wander through life, seeking worldly joys. I'd gotten where I wanted to be, but I still had no happiness, no peace of mind and no joy.

"I would always get hand claps, but I was miserable," he continued. "I went on the floor before the biggest crowd in basketball history and we beat UCLA and I was miserable."

That was in the Houston Astrodome when Hayes, playing for the University of Houston, beat college basketball's best team and its big center, Kareem Abdul-Jabbar, who was known as Lew Alcindor in those days. It should have been the height of accomplishment for Hayes, but nothing he did seemed to satisfy him.

"You get frustrated because you have no peace of mind," he said. "Then you get angry on the court and it costs you $50 for a technical foul. Then you lose your concentration."

With his religious awakening, the problems disappeared for Hayes. "Now I don't have a wandering mind," said the Big E. Jesus is victory. You never lose when you have Him."

The change in Hayes last season was dramatic. Saddled with a reputation as a problem child, he did a complete about-face and was Coach K.C. Jones' most consistent performer and the acknowledged leader of the Bullets. "I don't know where we would have been without him," said Jones. With him, Capital won the Central Division championship by 12 games as Hayes averaged 21.4 points per game and led the league with 18.1 rebounds per game. He also was No. 5 in the league with 240 blocked shots.

During the playoffs, he almost single-handedly forced Capital's opening round series against New York to the seven-game limit. For the first six games, he averaged more than 28 points and 16 rebounds per game and shot 56.5% from the field. In the seventh and decisive game, however, he came up virtually empty, managing only 12 points.

"It was a bad game," he said. "Just mark it off. If you base a whole season on just one game, that's not basketball. I played 82 games this season and seven playoff games. If you base what I did on one game, then you're a hypocrite."

There was no anger in Hayes' voice. He answered the questions in calm, measured tones. He was making no excuses for his performance, but rather trying to explain it. In the other dressing room, the Knicks' Walt Frazier appreciated his opponent.

"The man did all he could," said Frazier. "He had to be tired. He played almost every minute of every game. You don't think you're tired, you just don't do the things you normally do. The mind is willing but the body isn't. Too many minutes. It caught up with him."

"Stars always come under that kind of scrutiny," suggested Coach K.C. Jones. "Particularly when you lose."

Maybe that explains what happened to Hayes during

his early NBA years with the San Diego and Houston Rockets. The team was a frequent loser and the blame always seemed to be placed at Hayes' doorstep.

If the Rockets won, it was in spite of Hayes. If they lost, it was because of him. When Coach Jack McMahon was fired, Hayes was blamed. When Coach Alex Hannum was fired, Hayes was blamed again.

The worst time was under McMahon. Hayes will tell you that the coach made him the scapegoat for a poor team's problems. "Jack was always putting the rap on me," he said. "He would be buzzing in a corner with the writers, and they'd all just come looking to do me in."

Elvin sought various ways of expressing his distress. At one point, he shaved his head as a personal protest against the conditions in San Diego. His stomach was constantly knotted up from the tensions and pressures. "I would be calling the doctor at two in the morning like I was going to die or something. I was yelling at my wife and kids all day. All this pressure was just on me—and then they expected me to go out there and perform 100%. Man, all I wanted to do was get away. The club's owner, Bob Breitbart, talked me out of quitting a couple of times," Hayes said.

The Big E insists it wasn't his fault that McMahon was dismissed. He laughs at the recollection now but he wasn't laughing then. "Did I fire him at Cincinnati? At Chicago? At Pittsburgh of the ABA? The man was losing wherever he went."

Little changed under McMahon's successor, Hannum. Hayes was under a constant magnifying glass, his every move scrutinized and criticized. "He was one of the lowest, most conceited people I've ever seen," said Hayes, who never hid his dislike for either of his first two professional coaches. When financial problems forced the franchise to switch from San Diego to Houston, the new coach was Tex Winter. "Tex just didn't know what he wanted me to do," said Hayes. "He told me to stop shooting completely. I was supposed to become a passer. I could have done more for the team selling peanuts."

Eventually, Hayes was traded to the Bullets in exchange for Jack Marin. Coach Gene Shue had Wes Unseld playing center and so Hayes moved to forward with the Bullets. It made life considerably easier for him. "He [Unseld] took all the rebounding pressure off Elvin," said Shue. "With Wes in there, Elvin could wander away from the basket and do other things. When he did go to the boards, he didn't have to fight two or three opponents. And Elvin's attitude was just great. I don't understand how he got that bad reputation. He was an angel."

Hayes smiled at his ex-coach's reference to him being an angel. "Some will say I'm a religious fanatic," he said. "OK, I'll be a religious fanatic. I love the Lord. I just praise God and thank Him for what He has done to me, how He can make you a new creature. I know He's real, because He lives in me."

SPENCER HAYWOOD

When Bill Russell moved in as combination coach and general manager of the Seattle SuperSonics last season, he began two ambitious projects. One was to resurrect the sorry Sonics from a crestfallen to a contending National Basketball Association club. The other was to convert Spencer Haywood from forward to center. Excellent progress was recorded in both areas.

The Sonics finished with 10 more victories than they had the year before and moved from 34 games behind the division leader in 1972-73 to a more manageable 11-game deficit last season. There could be few complaints about that part of Russell's job.

But Haywood slipped from a 29.2 point per game average, third best in the league in 1972-73, to 23.5 last season. Does that mean that the other half of Russell's task didn't work out well? Don't you believe it.

"It will be a difficult transition to make," said Russell, "but it is necessary and vital for the team to win. I have no doubts that he will be able to adjust to the job. Already, his defense has improved and he's controlling the middle better. He has the size and capability to be among the best centers in the NBA. Offensively, he'll be able to take the big centers outside and the little center inside. At either spot, he's impossible to stop."

Certainly, Haywood has a pretty good teacher. Russell had been known to attract a few compliments for his work as an NBA center some years ago with the Boston Celtics. "He was," offers Haywood, "the greatest defensive center ever to have played the game." He was also a highly rated coach of the Celtics.

The major ingredient that Russell has going for him in attempting to make Haywood's conversion to center successful is Spencer's tremendous pride. Haywood is an intense individual who wants to be the best big man in basketball, Kareem Abdul-Jabbar notwithstanding.

"As long as Kareem is around, that's impossible, I guess," said Haywood, whose face bears a striking resemblance to that of comedian Bill Cosby. "But I'm still going to try. I want to be the best. I want to be the Most Valuable Player and help win a lot of championships."

There are some people who will tell you that Haywood should have been named the Most Valuable Player in the NBA All Star game last January. Playing on his home court, the Seattle Coliseum, Haywood enjoyed a super game. He scored 23 points, pulled down 11 rebounds and earned five assists in the West's 134-123 victory over the East. But Bob Lanier scored 24 with 10 rebounds. It was obvious that the MVP vote of the basketball writers present would be a struggle between the two young giants.

As Commissioner Walter Kennedy moved towards center court for the post-game presentation, he observed, "I may have to fight my way out of this Coliseum, if Haywood doesn't win."

The winner was Lanier and the cordial capacity Seattle crowd of more than 14,000 fans gave him a warm ovation despite the slighting of Haywood. Spencer didn't take it nearly as well.

"I thought I played up to the capacity to be selected," he said. "I hate to be in a league where I can't get the recognition."

Haywood got plenty of recognition in his first professional season. That was 1969-70 when he signed with the Denver Rockets of the American Basketball Association and led the league in scoring with an average of 30 points per game. He was named Rookie of the Year as well as Most Valuable Player in the league, a rather rare double award.

But the other league was beckoning and Haywood couldn't help listening. "I had been approached by some NBA owners with good, secure offers, and I really wanted to play in the NBA." Seattle won the bidding derby with a $1,500,000 package for six years. The deal was put together by Haywood's attorney, Al Ross, and SuperSonics' owner Sam Schulman. Denver, naturally, sued and the legal tug of war began.

"Those days were really rough," remembered Haywood. "I wasn't playing well and my mind wasn't on the game. I wasn't receiving any help from the players around the league. In fact, a lot of the players resented my causing such a ruckus."

Eventually, the legal matters were settled and Haywood had a home. "I want to play for Seattle for the rest of my career," he said. "All I want to do is play ball and earn my money."

Opponents say the 6-foot-8, 225-pound Haywood has nothing to worry about in that department. He has had some awesome games. One of the best was a 51-point performance against Kansas City-Omaha one night. Bob Cousy, then coach of the KC-Omaha club, was tremendously impressed.

"Haywood could become the greatest forward ever to play the game," said Cousy. "He has no glaring weakness. He looks for the opening he wants and he always seems to find it. With more experience, he'll find it more quickly. Yes, he could be the greatest forward ever."

Dave DeBusschere, who retired as a New York Knicks player last April, often matched up against Haywood in both the NBA and on the playground courts of Detroit, where Spencer refined his basketball. "He was a strong kid even then," remembered DeBusschere. "But now he's so fluid. He does everything so well. He glides and, physically, he's so much stronger."

Haywood was born in Silver City, Mississippi, one of 10 children. The family lived in a six-room house, often doubling and tripling up in the available beds. Spencer's mother mopped floors for extra money and her children did everything and anything to earn a few dollars. At various times, Spencer picked cotton, mowed lawns, worked as a caddy and even cut hair to help out.

When Spencer was a teen-ager, he moved to Detroit, joining an older brother, LeRoy. It was LeRoy who introduced Spencer to Will Robinson, the basketball coach at Pershing High School. And it was Robinson who helped Haywood out. He became the boy's guardian and saw to it that he was provided with a good home by some friends, James and Ida Bell. "They put me on the right road," said Haywood. "They told me it was sad to see a lot of talent go down the drain."

So Spencer decided to put a stopper in that drain. He broke away from the bad crowd he had been associating with and began concentrating instead on basketball. He starred for Robinson's team at Pershing High School and Coach Robinson encouraged the youngster to attend summer school to improve his chances for a collegiate career.

Haywood went from high school to tiny Trinidad Junior College in Colorado and emerged in the summer of 1968 as a national hero. That was the year of the Olympic basketball boycott by some of the nation's top collegiate players.

Haywood stepped into the spotlight, leading the United States to the Olympic gold medal.

He returned home for a year of college ball at the University of Detroit, where he earned All America honors. Then it was off to the pros, first at Denver and then with Seattle. Despite his almost instant success, Haywood has never forgotten his humble beginnings and the help he received along the way from people like Will Robinson and the Bells.

"I owe all my success to people and I want to help other people," he said. "If it wasn't for what certain people did for me along the way, I wouldn't be doing what I am now."

Now that he has achieved personal success, Haywood seeks the same goal for his team. "I've achieved a lot for a young player, but now I want to see my team win a championship," he said. "My career in the NBA won't be complete until I can help my team win the big one."

His coach, Bill Russell, has the same ambition.

DAN ISSEL

Consistency, thy name is Dan Issel.

Issel has been in the American Basketball Association four years. For the last three of those seasons, he has been the league's third best scorer. The only year he missed that position was 1970-71. That year, his first as a pro, Issel was the ABA's No. 1 scorer.

Since then, the names ahead of him in the final scoring figures have changed, but Issel remains, year in and year out, a pillar of consistency.

Yet Issel is considered the No. 2 weapon in the arsenal of the Kentucky Colonels. No. 1, of course, is Artis Gilmore, whose arrival in Kentucky one year after Issel's moved Dan out of his accustomed center slot to forward. The switch hasn't disturbed Issel in the least.

Dan came out of the University of Kentucky in 1970 as a center. He had broken or shared 41 collegiate records at UK as a center, and he accepted an estimated $1,400,000 Kentucky Colonel bonus as a center. He led all ABA scorers with a 29.9 scoring average and shared Rookie of the Year honors with Charlie Scott. The next thing he knew, Kentucky was drafting Gilmore, who at 7-foot-2 is, of course, a center. Issel got the message.

"I knew that the Colonels had picked the best college player in America to fit their particular needs," said Issel, reflecting on the drafting of Gilmore. That particular need was defensive. For as good a scorer as Issel is, he will never be confused with a defensive intimidator.

"My major contribution," said Issel straightforwardly, "is on offense." And on defense, Issel realized what a giant like Gilmore could mean to the Colonels under the basket. "It's a nice thought to know that a 7-foot-2-inch human eraser is going to be back there waiting for them if they get by me."

So Issel readily switched from center to forward and his productivity did not suffer one bit. If anything, he flourished because the burden of battling the league's giants had been lifted off his broad shoulders.

"I wasn't the intimidating player you need at center," he said. "My teammates had to spend a lot of time covering up for me. And because I wasn't able to do what a guy like Artis can do, the rest of the team had to play half a step farther off their men than they'd have liked. And that certainly didn't help our defense any."

Issel never felt any particular pressure in shifting from center to forward, discarding the position he had played through college for a brand new one that he had to learn from scratch. "I've been proving myself ever since I first put on a basketball uniform," he said.

That was back in Batavia, Illinois, where he was born. The game has been one of peaks and valleys for him, and they started back in grade school.

"After starting for my seventh grade team, I was benched in the eighth grade," he recalled. "Probably I can thank my father that I am still playing basketball after that happened. Even though he knew we'd have to be way ahead or hopelessly behind before he'd get to see me play, he still kept taking time off from work to come and watch the team. No pressure or anything. He was just always there. I guess I felt like I couldn't let him down."

Issel maneuvered his way out of that valley and played himself back into the starting lineup by the time he got to high school. When he was a senior, he averaged 26 points per game, was recognized as a high school All American and had the scouts beating a steady path to his door. Among them was the persuasive Baron of the Bluegrass, Coach Adolph Rupp of Kentucky.

Rupp, as anyone who has ever dealt with the Baron can tell you, was persuasive, but not quite persuasive enough. Kentucky almost lost Issel.

"I liked Wisconsin best," said Dan, "but my parents were impressed with the academic standing of Northwestern and wanted me to go there. I signed a Big Ten letter of intent, but I wasn't too hot on Northwestern."

Eventually, a compromise was reached and the winner turned out to be Rupp. Or was he? Suddenly, Issel dipped into another basketball valley. He was shockingly unimpressive at the start of his sophomore year. The big guy, it seemed, couldn't do anything right. He was beginning to look like a 6-foot-9-inch lemon.

"It would have been easy for Coach Rupp to bench me and go with someone else," said Issel. "And if he had, I might never have made it back into the lineup. But he didn't. He stuck with me. And by the second half of the season, I had begun to get straightened out."

For an example of the nightmare Issel lived through in those early varsity days, consider that in a game against Georgia, he played 25 minutes and produced the distinctly un-Issel-like statistics of two shots taken, no points scored, and two rebounds.

Somehow, Issel emerged from those doldrums and finished that first varsity season with a reasonable 16.4 average. Then, in his junior year, he began raising some eyebrows with a 26.6 average. He increased that to 33.9 as a senior and concluded his career as Kentucky's all-time leading scorer with a total of 2,138 points. Reaching that plateau meant passing some formidable predecessors such as Cotton Nash, Cliff Hagan and Alex Groza. Along the way, he also shattered Hagan's single game high with a 53-point show against Mississippi.

Issel had the good sense to be finishing his collegiate career at the height of the pro basketball war between the upstart ABA and established National Basketball Association. The ABA, always trying to get the jump on the older league, drafted first and Issel's rights went to Dallas. But big Dan had grown accustomed to the bluegrass and the Colonels had a better chance of signing him. So they sent a token check—something like $25,000—to Dallas for the rights to Issel. Then general manager Mike Storen got Issel's autograph on a Colonel contract for a cool $1,400,000. And Storen didn't even have to fight the NBA for Dan. He signed the big guy before the older league ever held its draft.

"I like Kentucky," explained Issel. "That's the big reason I signed with the Colonels before even being drafted by the NBA. And looking back on it, the offer by the NBA probably would have equaled and maybe even proven better than what the Colonels gave me."

Issel started slowly again. Another valley. In rookie camp, he was out of shape and looked it. "It left me with my doubts," he said, "but I knew I wasn't in shape. And I had less doubts than most people. If I hadn't had less doubts, I wouldn't have had any business trying to play this game."

Big Dan stuck to it and worked his way back out of that valley. The way he did it impressed older teammates such as Cincy Powell and Walt Simon.

"I've never seen anyone work harder for a shot than Dan does," said Powell. "He's taken some awful blows to get to that basket. But more often than not, he gets there. And another thing about Dan. You get in a tight situation and he wants the ball. He wants to do it himself. A lot of guys shy away from the ball when things get tough. But not Dan."

Simon called it determination. "He has pride, a lot of pride," said Simon.

Issel quickly soared to the top of the ABA scoring lists in his first year and he's been close to it ever since. It has been another peak for him, and he hopes it's a permanent one. So far, it has been.

BOB LANIER

They call Bob Lanier the Jolly Giant, which is entirely appropriate. His demeanor is usually happy-go-lucky and, studying his dimensions, there can be no question that he is certainly a giant.

Lanier towers 6-foot-11 and weighs a hefty 260 pounds. There is very little chance of him not being noticed under the basket. And during the 1973-74 National Basketball Association season, opponents began noticing Detroit's huge man in the middle, too. He was voted the Most Valuable Player in the mid-season All

Star Game and, if you ask Los Angeles veteran Jerry West, that was no one-night stand for Lanier.

"Bob Lanier," said West, "is the NBA's most valuable player this season. He's the most improved player I've seen in years, and he was pretty good to begin with."

Informed of the praise he had drawn from one of basketball's all-time greats, Lanier just grinned one of his jolly grins. "I'll tell you one thing," he said, "that Jerry West—he's a pretty intelligent dude."

Another time, Cotton Fitzsimmons, coach of the Atlanta Hawks, signed up for the Lanier Admiration Society. "He has the best shooting touch, inside or outside, of any big man I have seen in basketball," offered Fitzsimmons.

What did Lanier think of that bit of praise?

"He's right," said big Bob. "I do have the best shooting touch of any big man. I don't say that in a boastful way or anything like that. It is just a matter of fact. I agree with Fitzsimmons all the way."

That is most fortunate for Fitzsimmons. You'd never want somebody Lanier's size disagreeing with you.

In his fourth professional season, 1973-74, Lanier's domination under the boards and his expert shooting eye began paying dividends for the Pistons. He thoroughly enjoyed his year, not only because of his own achievements, but because for the first time since he joined them from St. Bonaventure, Detroit became a winner. The Pistons had the fourth best record in the NBA during the regular season and the man Lanier credited with turning the club around was Coach Ray Scott. It was no coincidence that Scott gave Lanier much of the credit for that turnaround.

"Scott taught us how to play good defense," said Lanier. "And he inspired us to shoot for a goal—a spot in the playoffs."

With Lanier averaging 22.5 points on a .504 shooting percentage, and 13.3 rebounds per game, the Pistons not only made the playoffs, but extended Chicago to seven games before being eliminated by the Bulls. Lanier also finished fourth in the league in blocked shots, ahead of such highly respected big men as Elvin Hayes, Nate Thurmond and Spencer Haywood.

"Lanier has really grown up this year," said Scott, as the season neared its conclusion. "He is having a fantastic season. He can do it all. He's overpowering."

For the first time since he was drafted out of college, Lanier played without pain in his right knee. He had ripped it up in the NCAA playoffs during his senior year at St. Bonaventure. "That knee hurt me until the middle of last year . . . and it interfered with my mobility. Now, it's fun to play again," he said.

Basketball had always been fun for Lanier, from the day he first showed up at the Masten Unit Boys Club in Buffalo at the age of 11. A strapping 5-foot-11 then, the youngster tripped on his way through the front door. How's that for an entry?

Three years later, he won the National Spot Shot championship, a competition calling for players to shoot from 25 marked spots on the court. Lanier connected on 23 of his attempts.

After that, Lanier and his size 22 sneakers showed up at St. Bonaventure. His roommate there was Billy Kalbaugh, a playmaking guard who remembers Lanier as "a really funny person."

Now there aren't too many things that you could mistake a man of Lanier's size for. However, at various times, Kalbaugh remembers Bob passing himself off as a soccer player and a boxer. "He loves every minute of being the real giant," said Kalbaugh.

At St. Bonaventure, Lanier spent much of his free time visiting the nearby Seneca Indian reservation.

Shortly before graduation, the Senecas held a special ceremony to make him a blood brother. His Indian name was to be Ha-You-Non-Da. Translated, that means "He Leaves Tracks." Size 22 tracks.

Lanier certainly left them at Bonaventure. In three varsity seasons, he set school records with 2,067 points and 1,180 rebounds. Bonnie Coach Larry Weise was always impressed with Lanier's team play. "I've never seen a more unselfish player," said Weise. "It may sound trite, but I would call him the complete basketball player."

That endorsement and Lanier's awesome size convinced the Pistons to make him their No. 1 draft choice in 1970 in spite of his knee injury. Then they outbid the American Basketball Association's New York Nets for the giant, signing him for a reported $1,300,000.

The bad knee slowed his early professional progress. Limited playing time produced a 15.6 point average and a bulging waistline. Lanier's weight ballooned to a totally unmanageable 290 pounds. During the off-season, Lanier went on a full-scale program to lose weight.

"I ran about a mile and a half a day and I ran the stadium steps at Wayne State University," he said. That acitvity was designed to strengthen the muscles in Lanier's leg. It must have worked because Lanier came to his second training camp at a relatively svelte 265 pounds. The result was a 25-point per game average and recognition as one the league's top young centers.

But Lanier has always been a team man and he was concerned about the Pistons' sorry record. "I would like to be winning," he often told reporters.

It wasn't until Scott arrived that Lanier began to realize that wish. Big Bob's first taste of victory came in the NBA's one-on-one halftime diversion for its nationally televised games. Lanier won the initial competition, earning a whopping $15,000.

With his development as a first class center came recognition and selection for the mid-season All Star Game. Surrounded by the game's best big men, Lanier barely made a ripple in his first two All Star appearances. Then came the 1973-74 game at Seattle and the big guy simply ran wild. He played 26 minutes and connected on 11 of 15 shots from the floor and pulled down 10 rebounds. He finished with a game-high 24 points and when they totaled the basketball writers' votes, he was the Most Valuable Player. When he arrived in the dressing room, clutching his trophy, Lanier, the team player, held it high and said to his 11 teammates, the best NBA players in the West Division, "You helped me win it."

One of those 11 was Dave Bing, his Detroit teammate. Bing smiled at the Jolly Giant.

"The big improvement in Bob this season is defensive," he said, "both team and individually. He's always been fantastic on offense. Next to Kareem (Abdul-Jabbar), he's the best center in the league."

There is one area in which Lanier already has an edge over Jabbar and the rest of the NBA centers. None of the others wears size 22 sneakers.

BOB McADOO

He never knew it at the time—he couldn't have—but the most important development in Bob McAdoo's basketball career came the day Wilt Chamberlain decided to jump to the San Diego Conquistadors of the American Basketball Association.

When Chamberlain lined his pockets with San Diego cash as coach and, he hoped, player for the Conquistadors, it left the Los Angeles Lakers with a gaping hole at center. For years, the Lakers had dominated the NBA's Western Division with the imposing Chamberlain bottling up the middle, under the basket for offensive and defensive rebounds and intimidating opponents on defense. Now, suddenly, as the 1973-74 season loomed ahead, there was no more Wilt.

The Lakers hurried into the trading marketplace, looking for a replacement. They didn't have to look very far. Buffalo had a promising young center named Elmore Smith. At 7-1 he possessed Wilt-like dimensions. And most important, he was available.

Quickly, the deal was made. Buffalo would break a cardinal pro basketball rule by trading a good, big man. Smith would go to Los Angeles in exchange for a marvelously talented forward, Jim McMillian. The trade solved Los Angeles' center shortage, but shifted the problem 3,000 miles east. Now it was the Buffalo Braves who didn't have a center. Or did they? Enter Bob McAdoo.

Now, McAdoo is certainly tall enough at 6-foot-10. But he's only a shade over 200 pounds and lacks the bulk that you'd expect a man in the middle to have. "A pro team thrives on tough defense inside," said Buffalo Coach Jack Ramsay. "It needs a big, muscular center." Lacking someone muscular, Ramsay went to someone big—McAdoo.

Big Bob had been the NBA's Rookie of the Year in 1973, based on 18 points and nine rebounds per game. But he did it at forward and often looked silly on defense—a large-sized 6-10 man often burdened with guarding smaller, quicker forwards such as Bill Bradley of the New York Knickerbockers, Atlanta's Lou Hudson and John Havlicek of the Boston Celtics. "It's obscene to watch McAdoo and Connie Hawkins match up," noted ex-pro Rod Hundley, now a broadcaster. "Nothing but a shootout."

McAdoo heard all the talk about his defense and, frankly, it bugged him. "I really shouldn't have been asked to play the 6-4 and 6-5 forwards," he said. "That's why I was labeled a bad defensive player. I was convinced last year I could play center in this league. It's where I've always played and I feel more at home there. On defense it keeps me nearer the basket where I think I can help the team more. On offense, I'm getting the ball more and I'm getting more shots from the middle."

Shifted to center, McAdoo responded with a first-class performance. He led the NBA in scoring with 30.6 points per game and also had the best shooting percentage, connecting on almost 55% of his shots. He was the third best shot-blocker in the league and No. 3 rebounder as well, in both departments finishing ahead of such well known big men as Detroit's Bob Lanier, Nate Thurmond of Golden State and Spencer Haywood of Seattle.

How good a year did he have? A measure of his accomplishment can be appreciated from the reaction of Laker Bill Bridges, who watched McAdoo with awe.

"The game is easy for him," said Bridges, a touch of admiration in his voice. "He's the best talent to come into the league in a long time. Maybe Oscar Robertson and Jerry West made it look that easy, but that's all. He scores 30 against [Kareem Abdul] Jabber, 30 against Thurmond, 30 against [Dave] Cowens. For him, the game is easy. He hasn't reached his peak, either. He will continue to get better. Just remember, the game is easy for him. Easy."

Should the switch from forward to center mean that much of a change in a player's productivity, though? Yes, if you listen to McAdoo. Playing forward, the big guy ran scared. "I was afraid to put the ball on the floor," he said. "The defender always had his eyes on my chest. I was used to looking a guy in the eyes and putting a few head fakes on him."

That's the way it had always been for big Bob, first at Vincennes, Indiana Junior College and then at the University of North Carolina. He had grown up in Greensboro, N.C. and after leading Vincennes to a national junior college championship, McAdoo looked around for a university. North Carolina was a natural. Only he never heard a word from the Tar Heels until it was almost too late. Finally John Lotz, an assistant coach at UNC, visited Vincennes to ask why McAdoo hadn't answered any of the school's inquiries. The reason was simple. Bob had never received them.

Once the communications gap between McAdoo and the school was bridged, he led the Tar Heels to five tournament championships and a No. 2 national ranking. He had one more year of collegiate eligibility left but passed it up when he was declared a hardship case available for an immediate pro draft.

"I began to do a little bit of dreaming," he confessed. "I was playing against good talent and holding my own." So the stringbean center signed a pro contract. Leaving college with a year of eligibility left, McAdoo caused a stir. His departure angered many irrationally, and taught McAdoo some lessons about people. He received batches of hate mail from those who were more concerned with UNC than they were with Bob McAdoo. There were the same kind of racial slurs that Hank Aaron faced when he dared to hit 715 home runs.

"I was hurt and angry," said McAdoo. "I couldn't

understand why they didn't want to see me with money. The white players were pretty well off. I was tired of seeing them with everything and me with nothing. I decided to get what I could."

At first, it seemed McAdoo might play in the ABA with the Virginia Squires. But he was underage when he signed an agreement with them and so he wound up in the NBA with Buffalo instead. There were times he was sorry he had ever gone that route, especially after a night of chasing those 6-4 and 6-5 shrimps around the court.

"It didn't take long after I was in the NBA before I was wishing I was back in school," he said.

"When McAdoo came into the league, he had the same problems lots of young players do," said Ramsay. "It takes time to learn and develop—at both ends."

Even though he often had his hands full, Bob did emerge as the league's best rookie, and that gave him something to live up to in his second go-round. "This year I had a lot to build up to," he said. "I didn't want to be Rookie of the Year and Flop of the Year this year. I really didn't expect anything like this."

It started with the first game of the season. McAdoo scored 31 points in that one, hitting 14 of 22 from the field, including the 17-foot jump shot with two seconds left in overtime that produced a 107-105 victory over Houston.

From there, big Bob kept up the pace, beating a steady tattoo on enemy baskets. "My confidence has developed the more I play," he said. "It began last year when I was able to play longer. You have to go through the league and feel out everybody to play good defense. You have to know what these guys like to do and how much they like to do it. I feel my defense is better and my offense is better because I've played more."

If you want to know about McAdoo's defense at center, listen to the Knicks' Walt Frazier, who says, "Near the basket, he's almost a Bill Russell."

If you want to know about his offense, check some box scores or the NBA's final statistics that showed him leading the league. Or, better yet, listen to the public address announcer in Buffalo, who has developed the habit of saluting each of the big guy's baskets by saying, "That's two for McAdoo."

GEORGE McGINNIS

If the world of professional basketball hadn't been put in a state of turmoil by the arrival of the American Basketball Association, George McGinnis would probably have been the rookie of the year last season. Instead, the strapping forward is an established professional star and one of the best front court men in any league.

Who says war is hell? Certainly not McGinnis, who took advantage of the basketball contract signing battle between the two leagues to ink a handsome contract with the Indiana Pacers following his sophomore season at the University of Indiana.

There are those who accused the Pacers of robbing the cradle by rushing McGinnis into the rough, tough world of pro basketball two years before he would have otherwise reached it. New York Knickerbocker scout Dick McGuire, however, was not among the accusers. "He was," said McGuire, "like a man among boys."

So the Pacers merely moved the man up in class, and McGinnis didn't exactly suffer. In his first two seasons in the ABA, Indiana won the championship. It was no coincidence. The big guy was the playoff MVP in 1973 after finishing second in scoring during the regular season with a 27.6 average. Last season, he was second again with a 25.8 scoring average behind Julius Erving of the New York Nets, and was the No. 2 rebounder with better than 14 recoveries per game, trailing only Kentucky's Artis Gilmore. That's not bad for a guy whose college class didn't graduate until June, 1973.

The thing that rushed George McGinnis into professional basketball two years before he otherwise would have made that move was the threat of a merger. Such a move could have taken away from young players any bargaining power they had because one league would have been bidding for their services instead of both.

"I felt the time had come for me to get in there before the merger," said McGinnis, after signing with the Pacers in the midst of peace talks between the two leagues. "My decision was financial . . . the future financial security of myself and my family. I am confident I can play pro ball and now is the time to prove it."

McGinnis, an aggressive 6-foot-7, had a sensational season in his one year of collegiate ball at the University of Indiana. He was the nation's fourth highest college scorer with a 29.9 average and he set a school record, scoring 719 points for the season. He also had 14.5 rebounds per game and led the Big Ten Conference in scoring and rebounding. He also set a conference record for most points in a season by a sophomore. He was, as scout McGuire observed, a man among boys.

It also didn't take Pacers' Coach Bob Leonard long to realize that McGinnis was something special. When Indiana signed the muscular youngster, Leonard was enthusiastic. "George has all the physical qualities to play pro ball," he said. "He has good size, is strong, can rebound, put the ball on the floor and move with or without the ball." After watching him in training camp, Leonard was one step beyond enthusiastic. He was ecstatic.

"If this kid learns the way I think he can," the coach said, "he'll be one of the finest forwards in basketball. It's been a long time since I've seen a fellow come in with his ability and physical equipment. We must remember, however, that he would be only a junior in college if he hadn't signed with us. If George had had two more years of college experience, I think he would enter pro ball ahead of Elgin Baylor at that stage."

McGinnis had a solid rookie season but was operating in fast first-year company. Other rookies in the ABA that season included Julius Erving and Artis Gilmore. Those two commanded most of the freshman attention, but insiders knew that Indiana's new man had the potential to be just as exciting as the others. And in his second year, he fulfilled that potential.

"There was no question in my mind that I had the ability," he said. "But I just had to wait my turn. It's different than college and you have to adjust. I was in a hurry. I wanted to do everything so quick."

His first year was a learning experience for big George. The lessons came from men who had been running up and down basketball courts when McGinnis was still in grade school. Men like Utah's Zelmo Beaty.

"You can't muscle all the way (to the basket), not all the time," said Beaty. "But McGinnis tries to. With George, it's just a matter of getting smarter. One of his problems is that he doesn't do what the offense or defense will let him do. He kind of predetermines what he's going to do. Then, in some cases, especially on defense, McGinnis doesn't use his strength as much as he should. He lets his man get him where he wants him.

He should push his man before he gets the ball—before the referee is going to be watching the two of them. But that comes with experience."

Once he got the experience and learned the little tricks of the trade, McGinnis began to resemble just what Coach Bob Leonard had said he would—a young Elgin Baylor. He displayed great body control and seemed able to stay in the air an extra instant when he got off his shots—much the way Baylor did. He was clearly blossoming into a star, noticed and appreciated by pro basketball devotees.

"Pro basketball actually is a show," said McGinnis. "You're on display. I didn't feel that way in high school or college. It was the greatest thing in the world to put on a suit. We'd just go out and play for fun. But now, it's a business. The whole object is winning. Don't get me wrong—I still enjoy it.

"I enjoy turning on a crowd," he continued. "If I can fire up a crowd by stuffing the ball or putting on a good move, I'll do it. It's not showboat. It's how I express myself on the basketball court."

Three years after he prematurely turned pro, McGinnis was asked if he'd do the same thing over again. "Looking back," he said, "I'm pretty satisfied with what I did. It's what I'd been looking forward to all my life. I'm not only doing what I like to do, I'm making a lot of money at it. Since the fourth or fifth grade, basketball has taken up most of my time and energy. That's the way it is for most serious players." And McGinnis is serious about this game, make no mistake about that.

"If a player is good enough to make money out of basketball, why not? Basketball is a short life and I decided to make the best of it when I could. There's no other way a guy 22 or 23 years old can make any more money and money makes the world go around. Everything in the world is based on money ... politics and everything else."

There were moments, though, especially when Indiana challenged UCLA for collegiate basketball supremacy two years ago, when McGinnis thought how much better the Hoosiers would have been if he had stayed in school. The fans noticed, too. But George had made his decision, and he lived with it. It wasn't so hard to do, especially on the first and 15th of each month when he got paid.

How much better would McGinnis have been with two more seasons of college ball? It's hard to believe he could have been any better than he has been. He's convinced of it. "There's no law that says you have to go to college four years to play," he says.

Especially when you're a man among boys.

THE ROOKIES

Professional basketball's 1974 rookie class includes the most exciting prospect in years. He is Bill Walton, a 6-foot-11 mountain of a man out of UCLA, spawning ground of many a top professional.

The red-haired Walton was drafted by San Diego a year ago as an ABA undergraduate selection. At the same time, the Philadelphia 76ers gained his rights in the NBA. He was wooed with bids that ran as high as $2,000,000 to pass up his final year at UCLA and turn pro. But Walton turned his back on the offers and returned for a final season under Coach John Wooden.

How could Walton reject that kind of money and

chance a crippling injury in college that might end the bidding for his autograph on a pro contract? After all, he already had been suffering with leg problems.

"I was enjoying school, friends and playing for UCLA too much to pack it in," he said simply.

That is Walton. A simple man really, wrapped in an enigmatic shroud of privacy. He shuns interviews much as his famous UCLA forerunner, Lew Alcindor, did. He loves his privacy and guards it zealously. "I'm not a public person in any sense of the word," he said.

Walton is a vegetarian who loves backpacking and communing with nature. "I love the beach and mountains," he said. "I like the outdoor-type lifestyle too much to give it up." His priorities are simple and basketball is rather low on the list. Asked what he considered the important things in the world, he replied directly. "Having fun. Enjoying life. Helping others. Being myself. Time, that's so important."

Perhaps his philosophy was best described in the short statement he made last January when he accepted the Sullivan Award as the nation's top amateur athlete. He was dressed in his usual outfit—sandals, denims and work shirt with rolled up sleeves.

"Playing basketball may be the thing I do best," he said. "I'm not convinced it will make me happy, though."

One thing that made the Portland Trailblazers happy, though, was the fact that they won the 1974 coin flip with Philadelphia for top choice in the NBA draft. That would be Walton, and it left the standout center with a choice of Portland if he decided to play in the NBA or San Diego if he chose the ABA. He picked Portland, signing a lucrative multi-year contract.

Walton had plenty of company in this year's rookie class. Other top prospects:

Tom Burleson, North Carolina State—Towering 7-

foot-4 center who has improved rapidly in junior and senior years. An outstanding rebounder who will be a great pro, according to N.C. State Coach Norm Sloan.

Keith Wilkes, UCLA—Sometimes overshadowed by Walton but a standout in his own right. Has pro-type speed and shots.

John Shumate, Notre Dame—Led basketball revival of the Irish with two standout seasons after recovering from a dangerous blood clot condition in his leg. Passed up final year of college eligibility to turn pro.

Marvin Barnes, Providence—Led the nation's rebounders with 19 per game. At 6-8, is likely to shift to forward in pros.

Len Elmore, Maryland—A bruiser of a center at 6-9 and described by Coach Lefty Driesell as "the best ever to play in the Atlantic Coast Conference."

Tom McMillen, Maryland—One of the nation's most sought after high school stars four years ago. He broke Gene Shue's career scoring record at Maryland. A big man with fluid moves and a sharp eye.

Bobby Jones, North Carolina—Hard-nosed defensive player who set all-time school record with 60% shooting percentage for his career.

Bill Knight, Pittsburgh—Key man for Panthers and considered one of the best players in school's history. A 6-6 forward with great shooting repertoire and eye.

Dennis DuVal, Syracuse—A top guard who is fast enough to run an offense. Good moves and a fine pair of hands make him a good pro prospect.

Campy Russell, Michigan—No relation to Cazzie but should be every bit as good a pro as his Michigan predecessor. Tough shooting forward who led Wolverines in NCAA tournament.

Tom Henderson, Hawaii—Fleet guard with dazzling

ball-handling and passing abilities. A first-class outside shooter.

Kevin Stacom, Providence—Ernie DiGregorio's collegiate running mate and considered in the same class. Tough defender with good jump shot.

Leonard Robinson, Tennessee State—Quick and tough under the boards, he averaged 25 points per game in senior year.

Jerry Davenport, Cameron State—Averaged 24 points per game and twice chosen Most Valuable Player in Oklahoma Collegiate Conference.

Clarence Walker, West Georgia—Scored 23 points per game and is considered a first-rate guard prospect.

PRO BASKETBALL'S OFFENSES

The X's and O's on the dressing room blackboard all translate into set plays for basketball players from the lower levels of junior high and high school right up to the sophisticated pros of the American and National Basketball Associations.

They share a common goal. The intricate lines are designed with one thing in mind—beat the opposition. Usually the beating is planned offensively with plays designed to free super shooters like Bob McAdoo of Buffalo or Julius Erving of the New York Nets for an open shot at the basket. But sometimes they are defensive maneuvers that will force the other team into an untenable situation—force a low percentage shot.

Basketball is a disciplined game. There are plans that must be used at both ends of the court, and most of those plans are diagrammed by the coaches and taught to their teams just the way they are presented here.

Those X's and O's translate into plays which, if properly executed, give the club using them an edge. That is what coaches are always looking for—the little edge that will put more points on the scoreboard than the other team scores.

NETS' 1-ON-1 FOR DR. J.

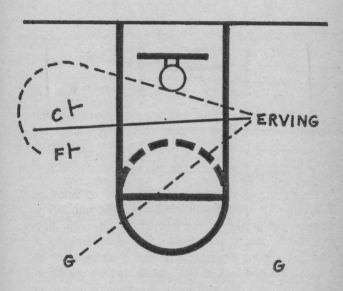

BROKEN LINE—Path of Player
SOLID LINE—Pass

The ball starts away from Erving. The guard's shuffle cuts off Doctor J. He goes around a double pick on the weak side set by the other forward and center. The guard with the ball then passes to The Doctor and he operates.

LOUIE DAMPIER'S THREE-POINT PLAY

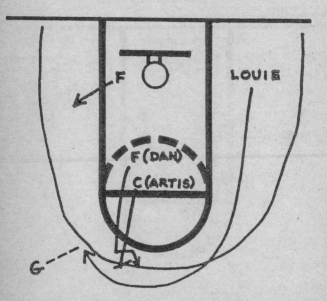

Artis Gilmore and Dan Issel come up and set a double pick. If Dampier isn't open, Issel rolls over the top of the pick set by Gilmore. This play is designed for a desperation situation.

KENTUCKY'S BIG A DEFENSE

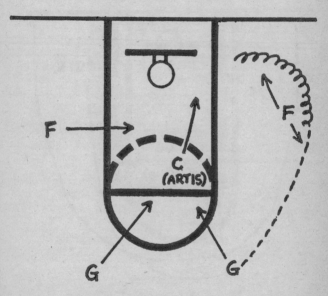

This defensive alignment forces the opposing forward to turn to the baseline. Both weakside people sag to the middle. Gilmore intercedes near the basket for the block.

UTAH'S "OFF BEATY" PLAY

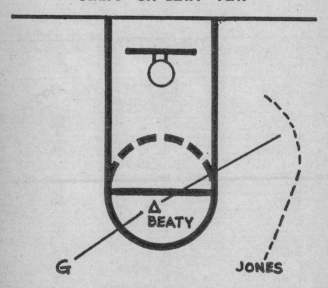

BROKEN LINE—Path of Player
SOLID LINE—Pass

A dominant center like Zelmo Beaty can create scoring opportunities like this one for Utah's Jimmy Jones, who must move without the ball to make it work. Beaty's pass must lead Jones for the break to the basket.

THE STATISTICS

ATLANTIC DIVISION

Club	W	L	Pct.	GB
Boston	56	26	.683	--
New York	49	33	.598	7
Buffalo	42	40	.512	14
Philadelphia	25	57	.305	31

CENTRAL DIVISION

Club	W	L	Pct.	GB
Capital	47	35	.573	--
Atlanta	35	47	.427	12
Houston	32	50	.390	15
Cleveland	29	53	.354	18

MIDWEST DIVISION

Club	W	L	Pct.	GB
Milwaukee	59	23	.720	--
Chicago	54	28	.659	5
Detroit	52	30	.634	7
KC-Omaha	33	49	.402	26

PACIFIC DIVISION

Club	W	L	Pct.	GB
Los Angeles	47	35	.573	--
Golden State	44	38	.537	3
Seattle	36	46	.439	11
Phoenix	30	52	.366	17
Portland	27	55	.329	20

FINAL REGULAR SEASON SCORING
(Minimum 65 Games Played)

	G	FG	FT	Pts.	Avg.
McAdoo, Buff.	74	901	459	2261	30.6
Maravich, Atl.	76	819	469	2107	27.7
Abdul-Jabbar, Mil.	81	948	295	2191	27.0
Hudson, Atl.	65	678	295	1651	25.4
Goodrich, L.A.	82	784	508	2076	25.3
Barry, G.S.	80	796	417	2009	25.1
Tomjanovich, Hou.	80	788	385	1961	24.5
Petrie, Port.	73	740	291	1771	24.3
Haywood, Sea.	75	694	373	1761	23.5
Havlicek, Bos.	76	685	346	1716	22.6
Lanier, Det.	81	748	326	1822	22.5
Wicks, Port.	75	685	314	1684	22.5
Chenier, Cap.	76	697	274	1668	21.9
Carr, Clev.	81	748	279	1775	21.9
B. Love, Chi.	82	731	323	1785	21.8
Hayes, Cap.	81	689	357	1735	21.4
Carter, Phil.	78	706	254	1666	21.4
Frazier, N.Y.	80	674	295	1643	20.5
Russell, G.S.	82	738	208	1684	20.5
Murphy, Hou.	81	671	310	1652	20.4
T. VanArsdale, Phil.	78	614	298	1526	19.6

ABA STANDINGS
(FINAL)
EASTERN DIVISION

Club	W	L	Pct.	GB
New York	55	29	.655	---
Kentucky	53	31	.631	2
Carolina	47	37	.560	8
Virginia	28	56	.333	27
Memphis	21	68	.250	34

WESTERN DIVISION

Club	W	L	Pct.	GB
Utah	51	33	.607	---
Indiana	46	38	.548	5
San Antonio	45	39	.536	6
Denver	37	47	.440	14
San Diego	37	47	.440	14

Note: San Diego won special game to gain fourth place and playoff berth over Denver.

FINAL REGULAR SEASON SCORING
(Minimum 1,000 Points)

Player, Club	GP	FG	FT	Pts.	Avg.
Erving, New York	84	897	454	2299	27.4
McGinnis, Indiana	80	784	488	2071	25.9
Issel, Kentucky	83	826	457	2118	25.5
Gervin, San Antonio	74	664	378	1730	23.4
Wise, Utah	82	712	396	1826	22.3
Lamar, San Diego	84	617	272	1713	20.4
Johnson, San Diego	84	657	199	1690	20.1
Carter, Virginia	80	529	392	1546	19.3
Thompson, Memphis	78	529	410	1498	19.2
Simpson, Denver	75	595	208	1404	18.7
Gilmore, Kentucky	84	621	326	1568	18.7
Calvin, Carolina	83	488	490	1496	18.0
Dampler, Kentucky	84	555	238	1492	17.8
Boone, Utah	84	581	300	1480	17.6
Jones, Utah	83	583	229	1395	16.8
Paultz, New York	77	519	222	1260	16.4
Kenon, New York	84	589	156	1334	15.9
Silas, San Antonio	84	486	349	1321	15.7
Jones, San Antonio	78	497	186	1219	15.6
Powell, Virginia	82	518	209	1275	15.6
Daniels, Indiana	76	478	211	1167	15.4
Jones, San Diego	79	505	171	1187	15.0
Chones, Carolina	83	535	155	1225	14.8
Eakins, Virginia	84	445	339	1229	14.6
Williamson, New York	77	480	150	1116	14.5

Three Point Field Goals—Erving 17, McGinnis 5, Issel 3, Gervin 8, Wise 2, Lamar 69, Johnson 59, Carter 32, Thompson 10, Simpson 2, Calvin 10, Dampier 48, Boone 6, R. Jones 13, Powell 10, C. Jones 2, Williamson 2.